THE POLITICAL ECONOMY OF BUSINESS ETHICS IN EAST ASIA

Elsevier
Asian Studies Series

Series Editor: Professor Chris Rowley,
Centre for Research on Asian Management,
Cass Business School,
City University, UK; HEAD Foundation, Singapore
(email: c.rowley@city.ac.uk)

Elsevier is pleased to publish this major series of books entitled Asian Studies: Contemporary Issues and Trends. The Series Editor is Professor Chris Rowley, Director, Centre for Research on Asian Management, City University, UK and Director, Research and Publications, HEAD Foundation, Singapore.

Asia has clearly undergone some major transformations in recent years and books in the series examine this transformation from a number of perspectives: economic, management, social, political and cultural. We seek authors from a broad range of areas and disciplinary interests covering, for example, business/management, political science, social science, history, sociology, gender studies, ethnography, economics and international relations, etc.

Importantly, the series examines both current developments and possible future trends. The series is aimed at an international market of academics and professionals working in the area. The books have been specially commissioned from leading authors. The objective is to provide the reader with an authoritative view of current thinking.

New authors: we would be delighted to hear from you if you have an idea for a book. We are interested in both shorter, practically orientated publications (45,0001 words) and longer, theoretical monographs (75,000_100,000 words). Our books can be single, joint or multi-author volumes. If you have an idea for a book, please contact the publishers or Professor Chris Rowley, the Series Editor.

Dr Glyn Jones
Elsevier Publishing
Email: g.jones.2@elsevier.com

Professor Chris Rowley
Cass Business School, City University
Email: c.rowley@city.ac.uk
www.cass.city.ac.uk/faculty/c.rowley

THE POLITICAL ECONOMY OF BUSINESS ETHICS IN EAST ASIA

A Historical and Comparative Perspective

Edited by

INGYU OH

GIL-SUNG PARK

AMSTERDAM • BOSTON • CAMBRIDGE • HEIDELBERG
LONDON • NEW YORK • OXFORD • PARIS • SAN DIEGO
SAN FRANCISCO • SINGAPORE • SYDNEY • TOKYO
Chandos Publishing is an imprint of Elsevier

Chandos Publishing is an imprint of Elsevier
50 Hampshire Street, 5th Floor, Cambridge, MA 02139, United States
The Boulevard, Langford Lane, Kidlington, OX5 1GB, United Kingdom

© 2017 Elsevier Ltd. All rights reserved.

No part of this publication may be reproduced or transmitted in any form or by any means, electronic or mechanical, including photocopying, recording, or any information storage and retrieval system, without permission in writing from the publisher. Details on how to seek permission, further information about the Publisher's permissions policies and our arrangements with organizations such as the Copyright Clearance Center and the Copyright Licensing Agency, can be found at our website: www.elsevier.com/permissions.

This book and the individual contributions contained in it are protected under copyright by the Publisher (other than as may be noted herein).

Notices

Knowledge and best practice in this field are constantly changing. As new research and experience broaden our understanding, changes in research methods, professional practices, or medical treatment may become necessary.

Practitioners and researchers must always rely on their own experience and knowledge in evaluating and using any information, methods, compounds, or experiments described herein. In using such information or methods they should be mindful of their own safety and the safety of others, including parties for whom they have a professional responsibility.

To the fullest extent of the law, neither the Publisher nor the authors, contributors, or editors, assume any liability for any injury and/or damage to persons or property as a matter of products liability, negligence or otherwise, or from any use or operation of any methods, products, instructions, or ideas contained in the material herein.

Library of Congress Cataloging-in-Publication Data
A catalog record for this book is available from the Library of Congress

British Library Cataloguing-in-Publication Data
A catalogue record for this book is available from the British Library

ISBN: 978-0-08-100690-0 (print)
ISBN: 978-0-08-100695-5 (online)

For information on all Chandos publications visit our website at https://www.elsevier.com/

  Working together to grow libraries in developing countries

www.elsevier.com • www.bookaid.org

Publisher: Glyn Jones
Acquisition Editor: Glyn Jones
Editorial Project Manager: Charlotte Cockle
Production Project Manager: Omer Mukthar
Cover Designer: Mark Rogers

Typeset by SPi Global, India

CONTENTS

Contributors ix
Author Biography xi

1. Comparing State Economic Ideologies and Business Ethics in East Asia   1
I. Oh

    1.1 Introduction   1
    1.2 Modes of Exchange and Ethical Persuasion   3
    1.3 East Asian Case Studies   7
    1.4 Conclusion   12
    References   13

2. From Market to Mode of Exchange   15
J. Lie

    2.1 Market   15
    2.2 Smith and Polanyi   19
    2.3 Mode of Exchange   23
    2.4 Agenda   29
    References   30

3. Confucianism and Work Ethic—Introducing the ReVaMB Model   33
C. Baumann, H. Winzar

    3.1 Why This Chapter?   33
    3.2 Values and Behavior: A New Conceptual Framework (ReVaMB)   35
    3.3 The ReVaMB Model Applied to Confucianism   42
    3.4 Confucianism in the Workplace   46
    3.5 Conclusion   48
    3.6 Implications and Future Research   48
    Appendix   51
    References   57

4. Corporate Authoritarianism and Civil Society Responding in Korea: The Case of Minority Shareholders' Movement   61
G.-S. Park

    4.1 Fall of the Myth of Corporate Authoritarianism   61
    4.2 The Unfolding of Minority Shareholders' Movement   64

4.3	Changes in Corporate Governance Structure	69
4.4	Corporate Governance as a Global Agenda: Not Limited to Korea	71
4.5	Conclusion: The Authority of Business Towards New Governance	73
References		76

5. Business Ethics in Korea: Chaebol Dynastic Practices and the Uneven Transition From a Market to an Entrepreneurial Mode of Exchange — 79

B. Dalton, M. dela Rama

5.1	Introduction	79
5.2	Korean Development During Mixed Modes of Exchange	80
5.3	"Our Actions are Justifiable Because They Deliver Economic Growth"	82
5.4	"Our Actions are Normal as They are Part of Korean Culture"	85
5.5	Corporate Governance and Business Ethics Post-Financial Crises	88
5.6	The Son Also Rises: Succession Planning in the Age of the Emerging Market and Entrepreneurial Modes of Exchange	89
5.7	Conclusion	91
References		92

6. Mapping K-Pop Past and Present: Shifting the Modes of Exchange — 95

K. Howard

6.1	What Exactly Is the Recorded Music Industry?	95
6.2	The Colonial Period to 1945: The Korean Music Industry, and Its Censorship Mechanisms, Emerges	97
6.3	Postliberation, 1945–1992: The Korean Music Industry Reformed	100
6.4	1992: Exploding Ballads	103
6.5	Packaging Korean Pop, 1996 Onwards	105
6.6	Conclusion	109
References		109

7. Business Ethics and Government Intervention in the Market in *Joseon* — 113

S. Kang, J. Choi

7.1	Introduction	113
7.2	The Principle of *Daedongbeop* and Management of *Seonhyecheong* in Late *Joseon*	116

7.3	State Managerial Ethics and Market Perceptions as Reflected in the *Daedongbeop*	121
7.4	Conclusion	127
	References	129

8. The Politics of Institutional Restructuring and Its Moral Persuasion in Japan: The Case of the Iron and Steel Industry (1919–34) — 131

P. von Staden

8.1	Introduction	131
8.2	Entrepreneurial Mode of Exchange: Survival Before Rationalization (1919–25)	133
8.3	Mercantile Mode of Exchange: Rationalization Gains Salience (1926–34)	138
8.4	Conclusion	144
Appendix 8.1	Shingikai Meetings of the Temporary Investigation Committee on Fiscal Policy and the Economy	145
Appendix 8.2	Background of Leading Members of the Temporary Investigation Committee on Fiscal Policy and the Economy	145
Appendix 8.3	Shingikai Meetings on the Japan Steel Corporation Bill	148
	References	149

9. Political Economy of Business Ethics in East Asia — 151

I. Oh, G.-S. Park

9.1	Introduction	151
9.2	Theoretical Implications of the Findings	154
9.3	Methodological Wisdom in the Study of Economic History and Business Ethics	155
9.4	Future Guidelines for Business Ethics Research	156
	References	157

Index — *159*

CONTRIBUTORS

C. Baumann
Macquarie University, Sydney, NSW, Australia; Seoul National University (SNU), Seoul, South Korea

J. Choi
Academy of Korean Studies, Seoul, South Korea

B. Dalton
University of Technology Sydney, Ultimo, NSW, Australia

M. dela Rama
University of Technology Sydney, Ultimo, NSW, Australia

K. Howard
SOAS, University of London, London, United Kingdom

S. Kang
Korea University, Seoul, South Korea

J. Lie
University of California, Berkeley, CA, United States

I. Oh
Korea University, Seoul, South Korea

G.-S. Park
Korea University, Seoul, South Korea

P. von Staden
KEDGE Business School, Marseille, France

H. Winzar
Macquarie University, Sydney, NSW, Australia

AUTHOR BIOGRAPHY

Ingyu Oh is a Professor of Sociology at the Research Institute of Korean Studies, Korea University. He is also the Secretary General of the World Association for Hallyu Studies. His main research interests are political economy, economic sociology, and cultural studies.

Gil-Sung Park is a Professor in the Department of Sociology at Korea University, where he is serving as the Provost and Dean of the Graduate School. He has been the President of the World Association for Hallyu Studies since 2013.

CHAPTER 1

Comparing State Economic Ideologies and Business Ethics in East Asia*

I. Oh
Korea University, Seoul, South Korea

1.1 INTRODUCTION

Marxist explanations of institutional evolution in human economic history have drastically waned over the years due to the collapse of global socialism and the rapid development of East Asian and other newly industrialized countries (NICS) economies, paradigmatic cases of the Asiatic mode of production (see *inter alia*, Giddens, 2002; Wade, 1990; Wallerstein, 2011). However, the ebb of the Marxian mode of production opened up an inexorable domination of free market discourses of "the end of history" (see *inter alia*, Curtis, 1995; Fukuyama, 2006; Marks, 1997; Palma, 2009; Williams, Sullivan, & Gwynn Matthews, 1997). The free market discourse also invited a new field of business ethics studies, where corporate social responsibility (CSR) along with ethical government regulations for business transparencies are taught to be Western in origin and generally feasible in mature neoclassical capitalism (see *inter alia*, Dahlsrud, 2008; Gjølberg, 2009; Matten & Moon, 2008).

Our understanding of human economic history, compiled in this volume, differs from these deterministic paradigms, as the authors find that different modes of production existed concomitantly in a given historical period. Also, macroeconomic institutions did not evolve from one predetermined stage to another, nor did they progress in dichotomous fashions, such as feudalism versus capitalism or capitalism versus socialism. Both materialistic and ideological headways in history confirm that progressions at one point in history ushered in regressions at the other without major exceptions, as our cases in this volume vindicate.

*This chapter was originally published in *Korea Observer* 45(3): 347–361.

To capture the dynamics of progression and regression in material and ideological worlds of human economic history, we propose to use the concept of "modes of exchange" first coined by Lie (1992) in his seminal analysis of British and Japanese institutional developments. He found that four different, instead of two dichotomous, modes of exchange, namely, manorial–market (intraregional trade) versus mercantilist–entrepreneurial (interregional trade), existed in early British and Japanese economic institutions (see Table 1.1). Furthermore, these four modes of exchange were routinely contested by power elites who represented different class or status interests, which were either highly polarized or highly leveled, within their own central and local political and economic institutions, and were either highly centralized or highly localized (fragmented). This new model of economic history exposes that the four modes of exchange existed concurrently even in highly centralized states with highly polarized social hierarchies.

The theoretical contribution of this volume to Lie's modes of exchange is adding a new theoretical layer of business ethics or moral persuasion to his model. Authors in this volume argue that moral persuasions preceded or accompanied confrontations among groups over the choice of particular modes of exchange in national and local economic institutions. The argument presented in this volume highlights that, for example, proponents of the market mode in intraregional trade during a specific historical period advanced not only the economic justifications of abolishing the manorial mode in favor of the other, but moral or ethical persuasions for the adoption of a new mode as well. In addition to the economic justification of efficiency supposedly epiphenomenal in the market mode, exponents of the mode argued that it would also harness fairness, purportedly a moral value, in intraregional trade. Therefore, business ethics is also a very fluid concept that has been widely modified by East Asian policymakers and scholars to supplement their advocacy of a particular mode of exchange.

Whether the modes of exchange preceded moral/ethical persuasions historically or vice versa is not our main question in this special volume. Our intention is not to engage in an ongoing debate on materialism versus idealism (see Béland & Cox, 2010). Rather, our intention is to show that moral/ethical justifications that occur concomitantly with changes in modes of exchange

Table 1.1 Descriptive typology of modes of exchange

Region	Open trade	Closed trade
Intraregional	Market	Manorial
Interregional	Entrepreneurial	Mercantile

were fluid in nature, with no absolute moral or philosophical value attached to a particular mode of exchange. For example, this volume finds that the institutional adoption of the free market and entrepreneurial modes of exchange would not necessarily necessitate a nationwide consensus that it is morally or ethically superior to that of the manorial/mercantile modes of exchange.

Having discovered this conceptual linkage between the mode of exchange and mode of moral persuasion, authors in this volume undertook year-long research and amassed empirical research results on historical and contemporary cases in East Asia with a theoretical chapter by John Lie. In this chapter, I outline theoretical foundations of modes of exchange and empirical findings each author has illustrated in their respective cases.

1.2 MODES OF EXCHANGE AND ETHICAL PERSUASION

As illustrated also in Chapter 2 of this book, Lie's (1992) concept of modes of exchange was a sociological attempt to revise the postwar understanding of the free market economy and its business ethics. A canard of the free market economy was its deliberate and consistent avoidance of defining the meaning of the free market under perfect competition and how it would actually work in human society (Lie, 1992). By not knowing what the free market actually was, studies of business ethics, including critiques of the free market economy ranging from Kantian ethics and utilitarianism to Rawlsian ethics, failed to criticize the perfect free market *per se*, as they focused on its imperfectness (Kant, 1997; Lie, 1992; Rawls, 2009).

Thinking within the parameter of an imaginary concept of the free market, utilitarian thinkers, for example, could not foresee or explain unintended consequences of the free market even with perfect competition. In a situation of perfect competition, for example, markets would produce goods and services for the wealthy disproportionately to the demands of the poor who would not be able to afford such expensive products (Lie, 1992). In a similar vein, Kantians did not bother to ask what the state could provide its citizens beyond the basic utility of security and property protection, although they correctly visualized certain absolute values in society that needed to be protected against individual or mass utilities (Sullivan, 1996). For that matter, Kantians would not take into consideration that the unregulated market would sometimes damage people's happiness and welfare despite the perfect market (e.g., environmental destruction).

Like Polanyi (1944), Rawls (2009) was no exception in that he conceived the perfect market as real and argued that his difference principle

would be realized in the perfect market, where firms would not employ market dominating behavior against competitors, allowing a complete decentralization of the market. However, it is not difficult to imagine firms' reluctance to decentralize their planning processes completely against the wishes of the perfect market in order to take advantage of the difference principle—namely, it is necessary that the government has to provide safety nets for the underprivileged from the market, and some firms would want to dominate the business-to-government market.

Instead of relying on an imaginary concept of the market, a sociological understanding of modes of exchange and moral/ethical persuasions "denotes an ensemble of traders engaged in commodity exchange under historically specific technological and socio-institutional constraints" (Lie, 1992, p. 510). According to the mode of exchange, "[e]xchange relations among traders [...] stem from the underlying dynamic of macrostructural change," which creates "opportunities for groups to construct exchange networks and to establish social organizations with an infrastructure, rules, and norms" (Lie, 1992, p. 510). Therefore, by highlighting concrete actors, their social networks, opportunity structures, and institutional changes within different modes of exchange, it is also clear as to who would actively promote or sometimes passively accept a particular mode of moral/ethical persuasion tied with the given opportunity structures, technological and socio-institutional constraints, and institutional or network preferences of a particular mode of exchange. In other words, the inadequacy of the moral critique of the free market economy by not being able to criticize the concept of market itself can now be supplanted by an alternative explanation. That is, moral persuasions are ideological justifications in tandem with economic reasoning in order to consolidate institutional transitions from one mode of exchange to another.

Conceived in this way, modes of exchange and moral/ethical persuasions are neither dichotomous (e.g., feudalism versus capitalism; capitalism versus socialism) nor continuous. It is often the norm in modern history to find the coexistence of different modes of exchange in one period, while movements from one mode to another are not always progressive but rather regressive. Modes of exchanges are fourfold, depending on the type of trade carried out by business actors in light of territorial and institutional restrictions (Table 1.2).

Table 1.2 Explanatory typology of modes of exchange

National centralization	Local stratification	
	Low	High
Low	Market	Manorial
High	Entrepreneurial	Mercantile

As the above tables show, four modes of exchange have descriptive and explanatory typologies. The descriptive one highlights the different business outcomes of the four types based on the patterns of trades (open versus closed; intra-versus interregional). The purpose of the descriptive typology is to identify major and idea-typical forms of trade that have historically existed in all human societies. The term "manorial" or "mercantile" therefore only distinguishes the open from the closed on the one hand, and the intraregional from the interregional on the other hand. The terms do not intend to include all regional variations that existed in human history, but rather categorize them into simple heuristic categories.

The explanatory one emphasizes different business outcomes of the four types based on national and local power structures (i.e., patterns of trade are dependent on different groups of business agents who are connected to different national and local power structures). The purpose of the explanatory typology is to explain historical movements and changes of the four modes of exchange throughout human history. Therefore this typology takes an epistemological assumption that modes of exchange move around different cells in the table based on power struggles between pro-market, pro-manorial, pro-entrepreneurial, and pro-mercantile groups. This occurs for both national and local power hierarchies, which are either highly centralized/stratified (mercantile) or highly decentralized/less stratified (market).

If historical movements are regularized, predetermined, or linear; market and entrepreneurial modes should not regress into manorial or mercantile modes on the one hand, and should not coexist with the latter on the other. However, Lie's (1992) historical case studies of the United Kingdom and Tokugawa, Japan reveal that regression and coexistence were both very common in the two countries. The chaotic progresses and regressions in economic history only corroborate the explanatory typology of the modes of exchange, that historical movement and/or changes are results of intergroup conflicts within given institutional constraints and repertoires (Elster, 1989; Hall & Soskice, 2001; North, 1990).

It is therefore only natural for us to assume that these intergroup conflicts over the choice of both macro- and microeconomic institutions must have necessitated moral persuasions in tandem with or prior to the usual economic reasoning. This does not mean that moral persuasions were used to complement economic reasoning. Instead, moral or ethical persuasions replaced categories of true or false with normative values of good or bad. In this sense, moral persuasions functioned as ideological garb for preferred economic outcomes in favor of a particular group or elite interests.

Table 1.3 Moral/ethical persuasions for modes of exchange

Moral/ethical persuasions	Modes of exchange	
	Market (Kantian fairness; Lockean liberty/equality)	Manorial (self-subsistence as ethical value; Confucian goodwill)
	Entrepreneurial (freedom to trade, innovation, knowledge as ethical business commodity)	Mercantile (rich state-strong army as ethical value)

In our case studies of East Asia in general, Japan and Korea in particular, proponents of each mode of production advanced different sets of moral persuasions (see Table 1.3). For example, to preserve a manorial mode of exchange, East Asian policymakers or interest groups preached a moral virtuousness of preserving the traditional vocation of communal and feudalistic peasantry, or suppressing evil vocations of profiteering and parasitic conniving in the manorial economy: the merchant class. On the other hand, East Asian proponents of the market or entrepreneurial mode of exchange presented a moral persuasion that the market (for intraregional trade) and the entrepreneurial (for interregional trade) modes of exchange would shield the moral and ethical principles of Kantian fairness and Lockean liberty and equality in terms of competition in the free market.

Among the types of moral/ethical persuasions, we notice that Confucian values and goodwill (e.g., filial piety) was one of the traditional means of protecting the interests of the manorial mode of exchange in Korea during the Joseon dynasty. This term is derived from the Confucian classics and refers to the stewardship of the Confucian state in regulating economic institutions on the one hand, and taking care of the welfare of its own people (baekseong) on the other. It is noteworthy that the Joseon dynasty maintained free clinics for poor urban people throughout its history, unlike previous kingdoms such as Goryeo.

The core of Confucian goodwill includes a particular incentive system awarded to peasants and merchants that would promote interests of both Confucian status groups so much so that neither could fail to embrace the incentives and defect from the system. As a consequence, some East Asian Confucian states, such as the Joseon dynasty, could maintain one of the strictest manorial and mercantile modes of exchange (or the peasant economy) over its 500-year history.

1.3 EAST ASIAN CASE STUDIES

The Confucian norm of filial piety still enjoys longevity in East Asia, and the moral persuasion based on Confucianism is effective in the region in disciplining workers and consumers. In a general empirical case that represents the Confucian regions of East Asia (China, Taiwan, Hong Kong, Singapore, Korea, Vietnam, and Japan), Chris Baumann and Hume Winzar propose a broad model of the relationship between Values and Workplace Behavior. The two authors propose a straightforward model where personal values drive behavior as illustrated in Fig. 1.1. Additionally, they posit that how much values drive behavior is a function of the circumstances in which individuals find themselves. Most importantly, values alone do not drive behavior, but the relative importance of competing values in different circumstances.

This empirical model of Confucian work ethic in the workplace proposes to investigate how macro-level norms of business ethics (e.g., market, manorial, entrepreneurial, and mercantile) compete with traditional norms of business ethics (e.g., Confucianism) among individual workers and business people in the workplace. The chapter shows how the Confucian norm of filial piety is more persuasive than its competing norms in East Asia, especially in the tertiary sector of the economy. The authors find that Confucianism may play a positive role in workplace behavior, especially when it comes to the provision of services (education, medical, transportation, hospitality, tourism, and retailing). In a service context, employee presentation includes the frontline employees' overall demeanor as well as their capacity to provide a smooth and natural flowing service experience. Service provision is often about providing accurate service, whilst maintaining a harmonious atmosphere during the service experience. Therefore even within the globalized market economy, the Confucian or manorial mode of exchange co-exists within the service sector in East Asia, making

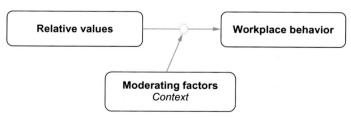

Fig. 1.1 Generalized conceptual framework: relative values and moderated behavior (ReVaMB).

it more competitive than its competitors in non-Confucian regions. On a macro level, this model also serves as a cornerstone for a Confucian state building and welfarism, which is explained in Kang and Choi's chapter in this book.

Gil-Sung Park switches the focus from Confucian discipline and work ethic to minority shareholder's movement in Korea. His starting puzzle is the fall of the state and corporate authoritarianism in the country, which has basically opened up a Pandora's box that invited myriads of social movements, including the minority shareholder movements that called for a massive reform of the Korean corporate governance according to the Anglo-American norm. What is peculiar in the process of the fall of corporate authoritarianism and the emergence of the minority shareholder movement is a new role civil society took up in the process of promoting and expanding their self and group interests. Park argues that the activist groups served the function of quasi-political parties in their place with political parties in Korea yet inadequate to represent the grassroots interests of the masses. The very lynchpin of Korean capitalism, a strong state with a Confucian hierarchy and patriarchy in the chaebol, revealed problems, "notably ending up serving only the interests and extended rule of those with power or capital." In other words, the lack of public sector mechanisms to monitor, criticize, and check state-business collusion eventually threatened the entire capitalist apparatus in Korea. The minority shareholders' movement, along with other Non-governmental Organization (NGO) activities in Korea, rooted in the Western idea of economic democratization, provided an initial step to resolve institutional chaos during a transition from an authoritarian political economy to a democratic one.

Given the persistent Confucian work ethic in the Korean workplace, changes in corporate governance seem a massive transformation in Korean society. However, Park argues that the owner-centric hierarchy, which had traditionally been at the heart of the need to improve corporate governance, actually showed signs of strengthening, still contributing much to Koreans' negative sentiment toward big business. Furthermore, the author issues a warning that it would be wrong to pigeonhole Koreans as being anticorporate, as "evidence on Koreans' enormous respect for professional businessmen and positive evaluation of large conglomerates' role in the economy suggests the opposite." This entails that Confucian values of respect and worship toward legitimate political and corporate power persists in Korea, reinforcing our belief that different modes of exchange coexist in one period.

Bronwen Dalton and Marie dela Rama pick up what Park left off: the chaebol and its succession problem. Authors start out from a very clear standpoint that competing institutional ideas and norms about how to organize Korea's economy in general or the chaebol in particular had coexisted since the onset of economic development in the 1960s. Therefore, for many decades Korea's economic and political elites have portrayed the leaders of South Korea's chaebols as "men of high moral standing, prepared to make whatever sacrifice is necessary for the good of their country—in essence as model nationalist capitalists." Countering to this common myth, the authors argue that new Korean civil society has regularly challenged this portrayal since the 1987 democratization. The so-called "chaebol legitimacy problem" has become even more acute, as the civil society and even the government are now attempting to put a curb on passing on chaebol ownership and wealth from father to son. Authors consider this case as an important case to which they can apply Lie's modes of exchange and his four typologies of market, manorial, mercantile, and entrepreneurial modes to understand the different interpretations of the concept of "business ethics" coexisting in contemporary Korea.

The succession case, for example, illustrates how new ethical norms of transparency and openness conflicts with the Confucian value of the first son succession. To keep the Confucian tradition despite challenges from civil society armed with Western ideals, authors find that "irregularities relating to founders' efforts to pass ownership onto their sons are likely to be more common in the coming years, as wealth transfer is taking place amid tighter controls." Manager-owners must now find ways around tougher anticross-shareholding laws while avoiding large inheritance taxes (eg, the heirs to the Samsung empire might face an inheritance tax bill of as much as US $6 billion). In this sense, depending on who one analyzes, Confucian ethics can be founded on individual or group interests as well, as much as it is grounded on collective welfare. However, authors also warn that some rules of the game are shifting and political and economic elites' past justification strategies are no longer working, as the Korean economy and democracy has matured and become more exposed to exogenous shocks.

Keith Howard focuses on another great transformation of the Korean music industry, from a closed and local music market with heavy state censorship and market control to one that fully embraces globalization and free market openness. Howard notes that the global music industry, which has typically been theorized as a recording industry, embraces and controls the creativity of artists while simultaneously seeking to influence the tastes

of consumers in order to generate profits. Although Theodor Adorno famously critiqued this market model, Howard argues that it nonetheless has primarily been a model that reflects the European and American industry in the mid- and late-20th century. However, its application today is increasingly problematic given the rapid decline in the market for recordings as physical objects.

The model also assumes a social organization of commodity exchange that poorly matches much of the world beyond Europe and America, including the Korean situation for much of the past and the present. Broadly stated, only the 1990s saw anything resembling the market model operating for K-pop. From liberation at the end of the Pacific War until then, partnerships between a censoring and controlling Korean government and a set of local recording companies and broadcasters had limited both the size of the market and the potential to generate profit. The emergence of transnational entertainment companies has reasserted control over artists, while forging new partnerships with a government now keen to promote Korean "soft culture" abroad.

Therefore, Howard challenges readers to consider John Lie's mode of exchange as a theoretical mind-map that offers a potential way to account for the past to present changes in the K-pop industry: from what emerged in the 1960s largely as closed trade commercialization based on social relations and power, then the coming of democracy in the early 1990s briefly blossoming as an open market, and coalescing into a mercantile virtual monopoly. The virtual monopoly in recent years has effectively leap-frogged the global music industry, as new business models are trialed that reduce the importance of recordings as physical objects. In this transformation, Howard concludes that ideas and moral/ethical persuasions of copyright protection or bypassing it through digital music downloading and streaming technology (all in legal fashion) have expedited its transformation.

Sangsoon Kang and Joo Hee Choi employ a new concept of Confucian goodwill to explain the process of ethical justification during the Daedongbeop tax reform in the 18th century Joseon dynasty. This chapter therefore can serve as an actual case study that discusses the historical origin of Confucian state building with a new concept of public welfare. In a nutshell, it is surprising to find out that Confucianism as a state ideology had intervened in the market to ameliorate problems of market failure. Defining the tax reform as royal efforts to defend manorial and mercantilist modes of exchange from the growing challenges of pro-market and pro-entrepreneurial groups within the dynasty, Kang and Choi analyze the

economic and ethical incentives of Confucian goodwill that sufficiently reinforced the traditional economic basis of the kingdom.

By alleviating the tax burden imposed on impoverished peasants due to wars and natural disasters, the government provided incentives to both peasants and merchants by opening up local markets to peasants on the one hand (i.e., market mode) and raising profit margins for interregional merchants on the other (i.e., entrepreneurial mode). The outcome was an egalitarian redistribution of national supplies of daily necessities to the urban poor in Seoul and the reduction of taxation for rural poor. The moral justification of the new tax system was Confucian in nature and highlighted its humanitarian principle vis-à-vis the efficiency rule rampant in the market mode.

Kang and Choi argue that the Confucian ethical persuasions helped the dynasty maintain the strictest manorial and mercantile rule in East Asia, even as China had to lift its bans on the market economy shortly before a similar rule in Japan. Although state officials knew very well that it would cost the royal family much more than either the manorial or the market mode in its pure form, they nonetheless experimented with this new tax system in order to suppress movement toward the market mode. It was therefore only a matter of time for the Joseon Dynasty to drain away revenue, causing a rapid decline of the kingdom in the latter half of the 19th century.

Finally, Peter von Staden takes up the case of the amalgamation of Japan's iron and steel industry (1919–34) as a case study of a use of moral persuasion in politics and economics. Located within the framework of a paradigmatic shift to the mercantilist mode from the entrepreneurial mode of exchange, the steel industrialists perceived the rationalization of their industry as essential to achieving greater national aggregate output. In its negotiations with businesses, the government employed various arguments at its disposal, both economic and moral. While the government drew on its mandated responsibility to realize national aspirations through industrialization, it was also a key stakeholder in the industry: indeed, it was the only substantial integrated producer. Central to von Staden's study is his examination of the politics of how moral persuasion is exercised by a government that was both arbitrator and player.

Does this lend strength to the moral argument or does it detract from it? Von Staden's findings suggest that as the moral argument was couched in terms of rationalization and that the government was the most efficient producer, it argued for changes from a position of moral high ground. But despite the government's seeming upper hand, for much of the protracted period of negotiation, morally based arguments held little or no sway over

entrepreneurs (and their firms). That being said, the moral stance did eventually gain traction as the economic strength of private sector interests weakened. Thus in the end, the shift to the mercantilist mode was aided by moral concerns, although the anticipated protection to be gained by the private sector under the new cartel was pivotal in the actual transition.

These case studies in one way or another accomplish the original purpose of linking the business ethics discourse to modes of exchange, the latter of which erratically move back and forth over the course of modernization. In a nutshell, all case studies confirm that business ethics narratives are strategically used to neutralize opposition to planned transformations of the modes of exchange.

1.4 CONCLUSION

When it comes to East Asian economic and business history, pundits are usually divided into those who believe that East Asian capitalism had sprouted out of indigenous socioeconomic conditions and those who emphasize that it was imported from the West in the form of imperialism. This seemingly endless debate is no longer pertinent today, as East Asia is a center of 21st century global capitalism, where the combined gross domestic product (GDP) of China (including Hong Kong, Taiwan), Singapore, Korea, and Japan is larger than that of North America. In other words, the wrangle over indigenous capitalism in East Asia is applicable only when the entire region under question is permanently backward compared to the EU, North America, and Japan (which the debaters consider had indigenous capitalism). Given the new fate of capitalism in this century, East Asia (and its culture and institutions) looms larger than indigenous capitalism for the capitalist success in China (including Taiwan, Hong Kong), Singapore, and Korea.

In a similar vein, the same experts are divided into a group that advocates a formula that equates indigenous capitalism with indigenous business ethics by emphasizing the absolute value of capitalist ethics and one that differentiates between the two, thus advocating a relativist view of business ethics. This debate has lost much of its appeal as business ethics has certainly become a universal concept in most developed countries, including those in East Asia, even though capitalist business ethics now embodies much of socialist or even traditional ethical values. What is more important than the absolutism versus relativism dispute is a new hypothesis that business ethics looms large during economic transitions from one particular mode of exchange to another.

Our case studies of East Asia in general and Korea and Japan in particular reveal that competing groups of policymakers and institutional actors utilized various ethical justifications to promote one mode of exchange over another, especially during transitional periods. When the public wanted stringent government control on seemingly unethical firms, corporate decision makers actively tried to coopt such exogenous pressures by utilizing conflicting versions of business ethics. In addition, these studies fail to find any systemic evidence to confirm the evolutionary hypothesis that business ethics, like modes of exchange, would also terminate in capitalist free market ethics that defend individualism, personal wealth, and political liberty. In East Asia, collectivism, national wealth, and political authoritarianism would have as strong a chance of evolutionary selection and survival as the capitalist ethos.

What these implications entail is that both material (modes of exchange qua institutions) and ideas (moral persuasions for each mode of exchange) matter in the economic history of institutions and it would be absurd to emphasize one over another. Further empirical studies on these thorny issues are thus called for.

REFERENCES

Béland, D., & Cox, R. H. (2010). *Ideas and politics in social science research*. Oxford: Oxford University Press.

Curtis, J. (1995). After history? Francis Fukuyama and his critics. *Canadian Journal of Political Science [Revue Canadienne de Science Politique]*, 28(3), 591–592.

Dahlsrud, A. (2008). How corporate social responsibility is defined: An analysis of 37 definitions. *Corporate Social Responsibility and Environmental Management*, 15(1), 1–13.

Elster, J. (1989). *Nuts and bolts for the social sciences*. Cambridge: Cambridge University Press.

Fukuyama, F. (2006). *The end of history and the last man*. New York: Free Press.

Giddens, A. (2002). *Runaway world: How globalisation is reshaping our lives*. London: Profile Books.

Gjølberg, M. (2009). The origin of corporate social responsibility: Global forces or national legacies? *Socio-Economic Review*, 7(4), mwp017.

Hall, P. A., & Soskice, D. (2001). *Varieties of capitalism: The institutional foundations of comparative advantage*. Oxford: Oxford University Press.

Kant, I. (1997). *Lectures on ethics*. Cambridge: Cambridge University Press.

Lie, J. (1992). The concept of mode of exchange. *American Sociological Review*, 57(4), 508–523.

Marks, S. (1997). The end of history-reflections on some international legal theses. *European Journal of International Law*, 8, 449–477.

Matten, D., & Moon, J. (2008). 'Implicit' and 'Explicit' CSR: A conceptual framework for a comparative understanding of corporate social responsibility. *Academy of Management Review*, 33(2), 404–424.

North, D. C. (1990). *Institutions, institutional change and economic performance*. Cambridge: Cambridge University Press.

Palma, J. G. (2009). The revenge of the market on the rentiers: Why neo-liberal reports of the end of history turned out to be premature. *Cambridge Journal of Economics*, 33(4), 829–869.

Polanyi, K. (1944). *The great transformation: The political and economic origins of our time*. Boston, MA: Beacon Press.
Rawls, J. (2009). *A theory of justice*. Cambridge, MA: Harvard University Press.
Sullivan, P. M. (1996). The 'Truth' in solipsism, and Wittgenstein's rejection of the a priori. *European Journal of Philosophy*, 4(2), 195–220.
Wade, R. (1990). *Governing the market: Economic theory and the role of government in East Asian industrialization*. Princeton, NJ: Princeton University Press.
Wallerstein, I. (2011). *The modern world-system I: Capitalist agriculture and the origins of the European world-economy in the sixteenth century, with a new prologue*. Berkeley, CA: University of California Press.
Williams, H. L., Sullivan, D., & Gwynn Matthews, E. (1997). *Francis Fukuyama and the end of history*. Cardiff: University of Wales Press.

CHAPTER 2

From Market to Mode of Exchange

J. Lie
University of California, Berkeley, CA, United States

2.1 MARKET

The category of the market dominates economic discourse. As the eminent historian of economics Blaug (1985, p. 6) put it: "The history of economic thought … is nothing but the history of our efforts to understand the workings of an economy based on market transactions." Even the leftish political economist Galbraith (1987, p. 25) declared that: "Economics in all modern manifestations centers on the market." Especially after the collapse of communism and the attendant end of the Cold War, the market-based economy appears as the only plausible basis of economic life. The currently regnant discourse of globalization is usually nothing but a case for neoliberalism, which is another way of articulating the same point: no alternatives but the market (Harvey, 2005). We are said to obtain not just commodities but also our jobs, spouses, and almost everything of significance in one or another market: market, market everywhere.

The hegemonic place of the market in economics and the social sciences contributes to its unchallenged status in contemporary politics and policy. Because our economy—called capitalist, industrial, or neoliberal—cannot but be conceptualized as a market economy, any other form of economy —communist or primitive—becomes tantamount to not really being an economy. Consider in this regard the destruction of a traditional village economy in Panama (Gudeman, 1978). The expansion of the market— what appears as the widening of choices and the coming of modernity for villagers—misses the more significant reality that it replaces and destroys the extant network of social relationships and economic organizations. Market expansion is not merely the construction of a new form of economic life; it is simultaneously a destruction of a traditional form of economic organization (cf. Hill, 1972). Like the myth of the virgin frontier, however, most

accounts ignore the existence of a network of commodity exchange before the coming of capitalist market economy. Just as traditional villagers are seen as people without history, they are also people without economy.

The sheer power of the market concept can be gleaned by observing the fact that Marxism—the most systematically articulated theoretical framework critical of capitalism—has been remiss in analyzing exchange relations and accepted the dominant theoretical conceptualization of the market (see, e.g., Boltanski & Chiapello, 2009; Dörre, Lessenich, & Rosa, 2009; in general, see Slater & Tonkiss, 2001; Spies-Butcher, Paton, & Cahill, 2012). The implicit equation of capitalism with market relegates all forms of decentralized economic arrangements as "bourgeois" economic forms. In the Soviet industrialization debate, market, and plan were seen as diametrically opposed alternatives (Brus, 1972; cf. Jones & Moskoff, 1991). In the name of centralized planning and socialism, the Soviet state purged petty farmers and liquidated traditional modes of production and exchange (Lewin, 1985). The horrors of the Soviet experience cannot be completely extricated from the impoverished theorization of the market. In spite of efforts to think about market socialism, the actually existing socialist states routinely reified and valorized centralized planning and castigated decentralized, unplanned market exchange, which allowed the state to suppress traditional or alternative forms of distribution and exchange (Kornai, 1992; cf. Lange & Taylor, 1938).

The point is precisely to transcend the false dichotomy between market and plan and consider more concrete social organizations of exchange. In this task, the received concept of the market is inadequate to account for the diversity of what in fact exists and is possible. Reconsideration seems especially urgent because the market concept, in spite of its ubiquity and omniscience, receives cursory examination in almost all works of economic theory and political economy. As Bernard (1977, p. 18) put it four decades ago: "The history of economic thought shows a surprisingly small amount of attention given to the idea of the market." The situation has not changed much since and, if anything, the collapse of the Soviet empire has merely emboldened the market concept into market fundamentalism. In spite of some recent efforts to rethink the foundations of economic theory, the vast majority of them avoid scrutinizing the organization and institutional constitution of fundamental economic categories (see, e.g., Akerlof & Shiller, 2009; Rodrik, 2015; Thaler, 2015).

What is the market? Friedman (1962, p. 14) symptomatically states: "Despite the important role of enterprises and of money in our actual

economy … the central characteristic of the market technique of achieving coordination is fully displayed in the simple exchange economy that contains neither enterprises nor money." Stripped to its core, the neoclassical conceptualization of the market exists without the appurtenances usually associated with its commonsense notion. It is a concept independent of concrete social relations or organizations (cf. O'Hara, 1995). Emboldened by an analytical fiction refined through mathematical modeling, economists, and other social scientists and virtually everyone else, frequently claim universal application for the market concept, from local transactions at weekly farmers' markets to dealings among transnational corporations, from the medieval marketplace to the modern placeless market. The market concept is applied to analyze Athenian *agora* as well as the contemporary global economy but, as Finley (1985, p. 23) argues, "to speak of a 'labor market' or a 'money market' is immediately to falsify the situation in the context of the ancient Greek economy." The modern idea of the market occludes the interplay of political and social networks that struggle to organize a distributional system, often to the benefits of the powers that be (Bresson, 2007–08). Yet the rare occasions in which economists acknowledge the absence of the market is only when they assume the absence of an economy *tout court* because their framework includes no other category of economic exchange. The neoclassical economic conceptualization of the market occludes the existence of qualitatively distinct social organizations of exchange.

The market concept is no more useful in analyzing the contemporary global economy than it is in analyzing the ancient Greek economy. Even the US financial market, which is generally regarded as the paradigmatic case of a market, diverges from the neoclassical economic imagery. It is a social organization that limits the number and type of actors and operates under conditions of uncertainty and political existence. The existence of social networks and the premium on inside information makes a mockery of the neoclassical economic assumptions about atomized individuals maximizing their utility under the condition of perfect information. Never mind that the financial market is a web of legal and political regulations and interventions, not to mention the ubiquity and the indispensability of information technology and other noneconomic factors without which it would cease to operate (Easley & Kleinberg, 2010; Knorr-Cetina & Preda, 2013; MacKenzie, 2006).

The limiting case of the financial market demonstrates the way in which the analytical fiction of the neoclassical market glosses over the social, political, cultural, technological, and other realities that constitute the disparate

organizations and practices of exchange activity. It blinds us to the distinct and heterogeneous forms of exchange structures and activities. The market is a theoretical black box in which its structures and processes operate outside real-world contexts. The theory imposes a particular structure to reality and in so doing it fails to provide a theoretical structure in which reality can inform theory.

Instead of treating the market as an analytical fiction, I proposed that we analyze exchange relations as a concrete social organization of traders, thereby treating diverse and distinct social forms hitherto obfuscated under the single and dominant rubric of the market (Lie, 1992). Thus traders and their roles, networks and organizations, rules and regulations, norms and customs, power and control, technology and geography, space and time, and institutional diversity and historical transformations become the object of investigation. In short, my proposal is for an interdisciplinary approach to the study of market exchange. In spite of numerous contributions by sociologists and other scientists to study the market since the 1980s or even before, we have not yet fully broken out of the prison of analytical fictions into the world of concrete social relations and structures, and attendant organizations of space and time (for overviews, see Aspers, 2011; Fligstein & Dauter, 2007; Lie, 1997).

The commitment to analyze concrete social relations and social structures transforms the constant of neoclassical analysis—the assumption of the market—into a variable, an object of investigation. The market is dethroned as a natural and necessary order. It is no longer considered as something given, but one that is made and remade, constructed and destroyed by concrete individuals and groups. From this perspective, it is possible to discern the structure or network of exchange relations, and to identify patterns of repeated transactions by a limited and relative stable set of actors. Elements that are treated as frictions under the neoclassical approach emerge as central characteristics. Uncertainty, social networks, geography, the state, technology, and other concrete facts of social life neglected in the neoclassical formulation emerge to take center stage.

Most importantly, questions of power and history come back into focus. Rather than treating the market as the only possible organization of commodity exchange, it is possible to analyze the birth, growth, and death of particular social structures of exchange or modes of exchange. Where the neoclassical approach only recognizes quantitative change, the mode of exchange perspective highlights qualitatively distinct transformations. In this perspective, the capitalist market economy that encroached on a

Panamanian village is no longer a simple expansion of the market to a nonmarket economy, but one form of social life destroying another. It is not adequate to characterize the market as a spontaneous and harmonious intercourse of atomized individuals. The mode of exchange approach presents all the dramas of social relations—including the social reality of power and control, competition and struggle, and collusion and cooperation—by networks of individuals with concrete interests and strategies to advance their agendas.

The agenda is to counter the dominant discourse that portrays the market as an abstract and impersonal force, as a natural and necessary arrangement of social life. I seek to debunk the naturalistic and necessitarian claim about the structure and practice of the market and to view it as a social organization created by people. The theoretical task is to begin with actors embedded in social relations, to consider organizations as corporate actors, to investigate them in the context of wider social structure and social and physical constraints, and to observe their historical transformations. In short, we need to explicate the structure of social relationships constituting economic activities in their proper historical contexts. The linchpin of the paradigm is the concept of mode of exchange: a social organization of commodity exchange constituted by traders under historically specific technological and institutional contexts. From this perspective, the neoclassical market concept obfuscates qualitatively distinct social organizations of commodity exchange and elides historical transformations. The largely descriptive task is to identify distinct modes of exchange. Furthermore, each mode of exchange is embedded in a larger social-structural configuration and emerges and disappears because of political struggles.

2.2 SMITH AND POLANYI

Whence the idea of the market? Almost everyone would point to Smith (1981), who wrote of "a certain propensity in human nature" which is "the propensity to truck, barter, and exchange one thing for another." Grounded in human nature, the market in turn has the endogenous dynamic to expand in absence of government intervention. In the long history of political economy, Karl Polanyi presented perhaps the most trenchant criticism of Smith's thesis. He argued that instead of being the cause, the propensity to "truck, barter, and exchange" was the consequence of market economy. By arguing for the political basis of market expansion and the embeddedness of the economy in society, Polanyi's revisionist account remains relevant

even in the 21st century (Block & Somers, 2014; Dale, 2016; Hann & Hart, 2010). Curiously, however, his criticism left Smith's concept of the autonomous and disembedded market intact. Instead, the embeddedness thesis should be applied to the realm of market exchange as well.

Adam Smith's influential argument in *The Wealth of Nations* remains the received view on the origin of market society. It should be noted at the outset that I present here a Smithian argument, rather than Smith's own account, which is much more historically and culturally bound than the received reading would suggest. The contextual account remains, however, very much a minority view (see, e.g., Hont, 2015; Phillipson, 2010; Winch, 1978). The presentist and paradigmatic reading has Smith beginning from the natural human propensity to "truck, barter, and exchange," which leads to market expansion and an increase in the social division of labor. In almost surely the most cited passage in the history of economics, Smith (1981, pp. 26–27) wrote: "It is not from the benevolence of the butcher, the brewer, or the baker, that we expect our dinner, but from their regard to their own interest." As a result: "Every man lives by exchanging, or becomes in some measure a merchant, and the society itself grows to be what is properly a commercial society" (Smith, 1981, p. 37). In such a society, the unintended consequence of self-regarding actions is to create a spontaneous but law-determined order where the metaphor of the invisible hand co-ordinates and disciplines the efforts of people in a harmonious and mutually beneficial fashion (Smith, 1981, p. 456). Natural human self-interest provides the ineluctable dynamic to the rise of market society. The only significant constraint is that the government ensure "freedom and security" by "surmounting a hundred impertinent obstructions with which the folly of human laws too often incumbers its operations" (Smith, 1981, p. 540; see also Smith, 1981, p. 343; cf. Herzog, 2013).

Smith presents the theoretical argument in the form of a hypothetical history in Books 1 and 2 of *The Wealth of Nations*. In Book 3, he discusses the concrete causes of the rise of market society after the fall of the Roman Empire when there was an endemic state of warfare among feudal lords. From the vicious cycle of sporadic growth and retrenchment, the breakthrough to market society occurred through the demonstration effect of exotic goods on feudal lords. That is, feudal lords traded their military prowess and political power for trinkets: "for the gratification of the most childish, the meanest and the most sordid of all vanities, they gradually bartered their whole power and authority" (Smith, 1981, p. 422). The unintended consequences of conspicuous consumption and pecuniary interest created

commercial society (cf. Hirschman, 1977). The theoretical fiction of Books 1 and 2 and the historical account of Book 3 both buttress Smith's denunciation of mercantilism in Book 4 and underscore his policy recommendations in Book 5. In order to avoid the wretched state of post-Roman Empire Europe and to maintain a society of liberty and prosperity, it is necessary to follow "the obvious and simple system of natural liberty": "the sovereign is completely discharged from … the duty of superintending the industry of private people" (Smith, 1981, p. 687). Here in nutshell is the case for *laissez-faire* economic policy.

Smith's conjectural history and the argument for *laissez-faire* dominate our view of market economy (cf. Lenin, 1956). Most contemporary scholars recount the gradual expansion of the market in a functionalist fashion, supplemented by an implicit teleology and evolutionism (see, e.g., Bateman, 2012; Epstein, 2010). The progress of the market appears as a series of solutions to the problem of attaining the theoretical perfection of the neoclassical market: perfect competition, information, mobility, and the *laissez-faire* government that protects property rights. The triumphant tale is usually embellished with a dramatic narrative of the victories of the enterprising bourgeoisie, the salutary effects of commerce and urban civilization, and perhaps an apologia for the woeful lot of the lazy and the rebellious. In almost all the narratives of market expansion, however, the idea of the "invisible hand" is taken literally and the expansion of the market is delineated as quantitative, cumulative, and homogeneous. The market remains a black box or an entity that is deemed so obvious as not to require description or elaboration. The motor of expansion remains from our transhistorical human propensity to "truck, barter, and exchange," which leads the market to expand gradually and surely. Revisionist accounts may introduce or stress an intervening variable, such as the rise of the state to protect property rights North and Thomas (1973), but the overarching narrative remains Smithian.

Polanyi's (1971, p. 148) fundamental insight was the embeddedness thesis: "human economy … is embedded and enmeshed in institutions, economic and non-economic." He criticized economists for applying categories derived from a market economy to study nonmarket economies. Yet, as I elaborate below, he failed to apply his embeddedness thesis to the sphere of market exchange and accepted the disembedded concept of the market. His analysis of the rise of market society focused on the impersonal process of the commodification of noncommodities. Although land, labor, and money are not commodities (which are produced for market exchange), they are treated as if they were produced for sale, which is

"entirely fictitious" (Polanyi, 1957, p. 72). From this conceptualization, he traced the commodification of labor, land, and money as the development of the market.

Polanyi viewed the creation of the free market as a utopian experiment in social engineering. The effort to construct a *laissez-faire* economy required active state intervention. "There was nothing natural about *laissez-faire*; free markets could never have come into being merely by allowing things to take their course" (Polanyi, 1957, p. 139). Market society does not arise from individual strivings, as Smith suggested, but rather from the power of the state: "The road to the free market was opened and kept open by an enormous increase in continuous, centrally organized and controlled interventionism" (Polanyi, 1957, p. 140). Not only do state intervention and regulation grow in tandem with market society but they also emerge by replacing a prior form of economy. The creation of a national labor market, for example, was tantamount to nothing "less than the wholesale destruction of the traditional fabric of life" (Polanyi, 1957, p. 77).

Polanyi suggests that market society itself created the Smithian theory of its development. That is, the rise of market society in the 19th century led to the discipline of political economy, which mistook the particular and exceptional case of the 19th century English case to be the universal and natural model. Put simply, the very idea that human beings have a natural propensity to "truck, barter, and exchange" was a product of market society, not the other way around (cf. Ubel, 2008).

In summary, Polanyi criticized the Smithian argument on the rise of market society on two major grounds. First, he argued that the alleged human tendency toward market exchange is a historical product of market society. Secondly, the rise of market society required tremendous political force. Rather than being a simple outgrowth of human nature, it depended on the active intervention of the state. In spite of the resonance of Polanyi's condemnation of, and moral exhortation, against economic liberalism and market capitalism, he accepts Smith's disembedded concept of the market. This vitiates his theory. On the one hand, the market concept only describes one form of commodity exchange. Because the market concept is viewed as a universally applicable and impersonal entity, he glosses over distinct social organizations of market exchange. On the other hand, he over-emphasizes the role of the state as the underlying motor of the rise of market society.

Polanyi accepts the disembedded concept of the market. He relies on the commodification of noncommodities as the indicator of the rise of market society. In so doing, he avoids analyzing concrete relations, organizations,

and processes of exchange. He is aware that there are different types of markets but considers them to be essentially isomorphic. In Marxian language, he accepts commodity fetishism by seeing what are in fact relations between people as relations between things. Polanyi's observation that the commodification of noncommodities is artificial or unnatural renders it a form of moral argument that leaves the category unscathed. By equating market with commodification, he obscures distinct social organizations of exchange. By tracing the homogeneous expansion of commodity exchange (a proxy for market expansion), he does not identify organizational diversity or historical transformations. That is, qualitative distinctions and transformations appear as merely quantitative changes. Consequently, Polanyi (1957, p. 58) dismisses local markets that proliferated in England before capitalism as "of little consequence," when in fact they were vital and significant (cf. Britnell, 1981). He overestimates the significance of market exchange and its purely economic character in market societies whereas he underestimates the importance of market exchange in nonmarket societies (e.g., Chaudhuri, 1985).

In accepting the market as a disembedded concept, Polanyi also exaggerates the role of the state in the rise of market society. Because the state is a social organization and the economy is not, he can see market expansion only as part and parcel of state action and intervention. That is, there are no social actors or social forces behind the expansion of the market. By rendering social actors, their interactions, social practices, and organizations invisible, we are only left with the master process of the commodification of noncommodities and the role of the state in it.

In short, Polanyi fails to carry his own insight to its logical conclusion. His embeddedness thesis can be applied to the sphere of market exchange. Indeed, Polanyi (1957, p. 72) defines the market as "empirical contacts between buyers and sellers," which would have offered a concrete starting point. The market is not an impersonal and automatic entity, but a structure of social relations and organizations.

2.3 MODE OF EXCHANGE

By unveiling commodity fetishism not only for the sphere of production but also for the sphere of exchange, the mode of exchange approach seeks to challenge the hegemonic role of neoclassical economic theory in describing and explaining market exchange. Beginning from the insight that social relations among people in concrete historical and social settings are

the proper objects of inquiry, it seeks to analyze historically transient nature of economic structures and categories. Beyond being aware of social underpinnings of all human activities and structures and their historical transformations, it also seeks to stress prevailing constraints of social forces or available technology. Mode of exchange is a historically specific social organization of economic exchange, denoting an ensemble of traders and organizations engaged in commodity exchange under historically specific technological and other constraints (see Lie, 1992, 2014).

Peering beneath the veil of the market—the black box of market exchange—requires us to visualize the invisible hand. Here the mode of exchange approach begins with Polanyi's (1957, p. 72) definition of market exchange as "empirical contacts between buyers and sellers." By ascertaining who deals with whom—to identify the actors and their networks—it seeks to establish the parameters of a particular social context of interaction. Atomized individuals trading with strangers on a sporadic basis is a historical anomaly. The stress should rather be on repeated transactions among a finite number of traders: a social organization of exchange.

In constructing a framework of analyzing historically shifting organizations of exchange, the mode of exchange approach stresses two dimensions. The first—social relations of exchange—refers to the dominant form of social relations within which commodity exchange is conducted. Its defining features are networks that exist among traders and their legal, institutional, and other infrastructures and norms involved in commodity exchange. The investigation focuses on repetitive transactions among a finite number of actors. The fact that some people trade whereas others do not may denote differential access to desired activities and resources. The freedom to trade occurs in a particular social context: trade is at all times a privilege and a terrain of conflict. This leads to an emphasis on analyzing power struggles among different actors and groups to seize control—or to establish the prevailing rules—of the dominant form of organizing commodity exchange. The stress on social relations and power struggles—and not just rules and norms—differentiates the mode of exchange approach from an earlier sociology of market exchange (e.g., Parsons & Smelser, 1956, p. 104ff).

The second dimension is means of exchange. It refers to the technological infrastructure and tools involved in economic exchange. Two main facets of this component are transportation and communication. Transportation includes the condition of roads and other routes by which commodities and traders move. Communication refers to the flow of information.

Both are deeply implicated in social relations of exchange and are conceptualized as constraints posed or possibilities opened by any given historical epoch. They thereby provide a historical anchor to the idea of mode and exchange and infuse it with realistic parameters of the possibility of interactions under a given mode of exchange.

There are no strictly determinant relationships between social relations and means of exchange. The latter generally constrains—as much as it may enable—possible arrangements of exchange. I do not imply technological determinism. The development in transportation capacity—think only of the railroad in the early 19th century in the United States—does wonders for commerce, in terms of both extension and intensity, but it does not in and of itself cause change in the prevailing mode of exchange (cf. Fogel, 1964; Wolmar, 2012). The coming of the Internet, to take another example, accelerates and facilitates exchange activities of all sorts but it is hard to see how technology by itself has a revolutionary impact on the social organization of economic life (cf. Comino & Manenti, 2014). In contrast, changes in the social relations of exchange frequently bring about change in the means of exchange, and therefore in the mode of exchange. The rapid improvements in interregional transportation often occur from the transformation in the social organization of trade.

In the original formulation of the mode of exchange approach, I stressed the primacy of social structure in explaining transformations in mode of exchange. By and large, macro-structural changes generate opportunities for individuals and groups to create and sustain new networks of exchange, and therefore to establish a new social organization of exchange with distinct infrastructures and technology, rules and norms. The larger social structure can provide the historical dynamic that leads to the rise of a particular mode, though its emergence can in turn affect the larger social structure. I am less certain of the primacy of structure, as revolutionary technology or even individual—though often as a group—can make massive changes, though often unintentional and unintended.

My reservation about the primacy of social structure is part of my desire to offer the mode of exchange approach as a conceptual prism or a heuristic device to investigate and illuminate concrete exchange relations and organizations. It is not intended as a master concept to apprehend *a priori* the different forms of commodity exchange. The point is not to replace the neoclassical fiction with another, sociological one, but to provide a framework with which to visualize social relations, social structures, technology, and other constituents of market exchange.

In my initial formulation, I presented a fourfold typology of modes of exchange (Lie, 1992). The first axis distinguishes between two types of social relations of exchange. The second axis divides intraregional from interregional trade. Together, they define four qualitative different modes of exchange. Needless to say, there are potentially other modes of exchange.

The first axis distinguishes two types of social relations of exchange: direct or indirect. In this framework, direct refers to cases where there is popular participation in exchange, whereas indirect refers to cases where a small group of traders dominate exchange. The crucial issue is the control over exchange activities. Frequently people are able to participate in exchange only through a highly restricted organization. Greater participation usually entails contests and struggles, and over time may supersede the older mode of exchange.

Direct trade refers to popular participation in commodity exchange. It implies retail trade, which is usually related directly to production. It is an open system where the social boundary of trade and traders is permeable. There is no entrenched system of privileges. Indirect trade refers to the lack of popular participation in exchange. It usually implies wholesale trade, which is relatively independent of production. That is, indirect trade often involves merchants who buy in order to resell. It implies a closed system where trade tends toward social closure and barriers to participation. It relies on private rules or norms of mercantile organizations or public laws of the political authority to protect and entrench its privileged status.

The second axis distinguishes intraregional and interregional trade. The idea of region is marked by technological constraints impinging on trade at any given point and time. Region is a historically variable arena within which regular exchange transactions are possible for the majority of the populace. Its extent is dependent on the prevailing technology of transportation and communication. That is, it is defined by the contemporary means of exchange: the better the technology, the larger the region. The crucial point is that there are technological limitations on the existence of regular interactions among traders. Region, in short provides the bounded arena within which market exchange is possible.

The shift from intraregional to interregional is qualitative in impact. It is no longer possible to have regular, direct interactions among the majority of the population. In interregional trade, regular transactions become possible only for a subset of the population. That is, it requires specialists in trade, who usually seek to establish asymmetrical relations between producers and consumers. Not only does the shift transform the interactive character of trade, but it also affects who traders are.

The *market mode* denotes a social organization of direct trade inside a region. Although it may take a variety of institutional forms, it usually occurs in a specific and specified site, such as a marketplace. That is, the conventional historical definition of the market makes sense: "A market is generally understood as a regularly-recurring assembly of sellers and buyers in a fixed locality and for a fixed period for purposes of trade" (Glamann, 1977, p. 266). The market region contains minimal specialization of economic tasks and no particular groups who specialize in the business of trade. It often serves a relatively autarchic region within which much of the production is geared toward either household consumption or local marketplace transaction. Consequently, trade is retail. Because the market serves a fairly self-sufficient community, the economic function of exchange is closely implicated in needs of the community. It also provides one of the chief means of socializing among community members. The operation of the market mode presupposes other social activities, such as festivals or rituals.

The region served by the market is relatively impermeable and ensures the existence of a relatively stable set of traders. Repeated and recurrent social interactions ensure that traders will know each other and facilitate the sociological basis of trust. The visibility of the marketplace transaction will deter efforts toward fraud and other attempts to undermine it. Therefore the market mode has a relatively undifferentiated role structure and a normative basis of trust. Smith was right to stress that the market made has a dynamic tendency to encourage division of labor and therefore to increase productivity. However, its extent is limited by the region within which it operates. It must transform into one of the interregional modes to expand beyond the region, which is largely determined by contemporary technological conditions.

The market mode should not be confused with the marketplace. The Wall Street—a synecdoche for the capital of global finance—demonstrates features of the marketplace, as transactions that seem to occur in a fixed site on a regular basis. However, it is in fact an instance of indirect and interregional trade. The superficial similarity with the market mode should not ignore that global finance takes place beyond any possible notion of the region and on a scale in which most people cannot possibly participate. Access is restricted, though there are constant struggles over the right to trade and participate in global finance.

The *manorial mode* refers to an intraregional trading system whereby the organization of commodity exchange is controlled by local elites. A small group restricts buying and selling activities. The manorial mode may employ a physical marketplace but the salient distinction is the nature of participation in trade.

The monopoly or oligopoly of exchange activities is sustained by squelching competition within the region and resisting the penetration of interregional economic organizations that are not in symbiotic relations with local elites. Since local elites direct economic activities—and resist both popular and extra-local participation—the mode tends to be static. The source of profit lies in extracting surplus or extending its sphere of operation. It is possible that the intraregional dominance of the manorial mode operates in conjunction with the interregional dominance of the mercantile mode.

The manorial mode may also engender an alternative form of the market mode: the black market or the underground economy. Given the control of local trade by local elites, the populace may engage in illegal or illicit trade. In due course, the popular organization may institutionalize itself, and possibly even supersede, the control over popular trade. Here again there may be constant struggles about not only the legality of what can be traded but also who gets to participate in exchange.

The *mercantile mode* is an interregional network of indirect trade. It presupposes concentration of resources to undertake interregional transportation and minimize uncertain outcomes. In order to dominate interregional trade, mercantile elites establish control within the organization by maintaining particular rules of the game and protecting their monopoly as well as to suppress potential competition. They are also usually linked to the central political authority in order to ensure control over interregional trade. Most commonly, merchants gain political prerogatives by providing financial remuneration for political decision-makers. Because the basis of their profit is the exploitation or regional price differentials or a monopoly over commodities, mercantile elites are deeply dependent on political protection that guarantees their ability to monopolize trade. There is thus a tendency toward collusion, not competition.

The mercantile mode tends to be static because of its monopolistic character. Efforts are made to routinize revenues and to decrease risk and uncertainty. In this endeavor, merchants often turn themselves into usury capital and rarely invest in production. The emphasis is decided conservative: to maintain their privileged role, they seek out new sites by the received method. There are, however, two outliers. First, the presence of an extremely successful mercantile organization may result in its emergence as an independent political power. Second, the existence of a powerful state may lead it to subsume mercantile activities under its operations. In either case, the exogenous dynamic of the social group representing the particular mercantile mode may render it dynamic and expansionist.

Finally, the *entrepreneurial mode* provides an interregional organization of direct trade. It is direct because traders connect producers to consumers or to other producers beyond the confines of a region. The organization of trade is open to popular participation and requires little in the way of privileged access or information. Unlike the mercantile mode, it is a relatively open system, albeit constituted by a specialized class of traders who undertake the task of inter-regional trade.

The entrepreneurial mode tends to be dynamic and expansive. When entrepreneurial traders are drawn from the market mode, they transform themselves from artisan-traders or farmer-traders into specialized traders by creating a network of artisanal or agricultural exchange. Because their source of profit is not in their ability to speculate across time or space as it is that of those in the mercantile mode, they must seek pecuniary pursuits through expanding or intensifying their operations. That is, they utilize existing commodity production and expand its sphere of operation. In the process, they may transform the process of production and bring it under their control. When entrepreneurial traders are drawn from the manorial mode, they intensify the existing social structure of the region by trading specialized produce and products across regions.

In any given polity at a given time, different modes of exchange may coexist. Furthermore, there are no determinate trajectories from one mode to another. As I have suggested, the underlying social structure provides the context within which different modes may exist, predominate, or disappear. Yet the structural foundation is by no means determinate and distinct modes of exchange may struggle to become dominant. In so doing, it may affect the larger social structure. The mode of exchange approach highlights groups of people constructing networks of exchange to advance their interests.

2.4 AGENDA

The concept of mode of exchange is part of a larger project of new political economy. At least three other modes must be considered to make sense of the totality of economic life in any social formation: mode of production, mode of consumption, and mode of regulation. They refer, respectively, to the traditional categories of work, culture, and politics. These conceptual prisms provide no one-to-one correspondence between different sites and practice of economic activities. The practice of exchange may often be inseparable from that of production. Furthermore, politics and culture both operate in the ostensibly economic sphere of commodity exchange.

Ultimately, these four modes should be analyzed as a structured totality of overlapping social networks and organizations.

The general agenda is to decipher the constructed character of economic life and its embeddedness in the fabric of social life. The initial step is descriptive: to identify social relations, organizations, technological, infrastructural, and related conditions. It is then necessary to amalgamate these into a unified picture of how a given social formation works. Visualizing the invisible hand is ultimately an effort to unshackle our social and political imagination from the ideology of the market—its bogus claims about the naturalness and necessity of market economy.

REFERENCES

Akerlof, G. A., & Shiller, R. J. (2009). *Animal spirits: How human psychology drives the economy, and why it matters for global capitalism*. Princeton, NJ: Princeton University Press.

Aspers, P. (2011). *Markets*. Cambridge: Polity Press.

Bateman, V. N. (2012). *Markets and growth in early modern Europe*. London: Routledge.

Bernard, B. (1977). The absolutization of the market: Some notes on how we got from there to here. In G. Dworkin, G. Bermant, & P. G. Brown (Eds.), *Markets and morals* (pp. 15–31). Washington, DC: Hemisphere.

Blaug, M. (1985 [1962]). *Economic theory in retrospect* (4th ed.). Cambridge: Cambridge University Press.

Block, F., & Somers, M. R. (2014). *The power of market fundamentalism: Karl Polanyi's critique*. Cambridge: Harvard University Press.

Boltanski, L., & Chiapello, È. (2009). *Le nouvel esprit du capitalism*. Paris: Gallimard.

Bresson, A. (2007–08). *L'économie de la grèce des cités*. *(2 Vols)*. Paris: Armand Colin.

Britnell, R. H. (1981). The proliferation of markets in medieval England 1200-1349. *The Economic History Review, 31*, 183–196. 2nd ser.

Brus, W. (1972). *The market in a socialist economy*. London: RKP.

Chaudhuri, K. N. (1985). *Trade and civilisation in the Indian Ocean*. Cambridge: Cambridge University Press.

Comino, S., & Manenti, F. M. (2014). *Industrial organisation of high-technology market: The internet and information technologies*. Cheltenham: Edward Elgar.

Dale, G. (2016). *Karl Polanyi: A life on the left*. New York: Columbia University Press.

Dörre, K., Lessenich, S., & Rosa, H. (2009). *Soziologie—kapitalismus—kritik: Eine debatte*. Frankfurt am Main: Suhrkamp.

Easley, D., & Kleinberg, J. (2010). *Networks, crowds, and market*. Cambridge: Cambridge University Press.

Epstein, S. R. (2010). *Freedom and growth: The development of states and markets in Europe, 1300–1750*. London: Routledge.

Finley, M. I. (1985 [1973]). *The ancient economy* (2nd ed.). Berkeley, CA: University of California Press.

Fligstein, N., & Dauter, L. (2007). The sociology of markets. *Annual Review of Sociology, 33*, 6.1–6.24.

Fogel, R. W. (1964). *Railroads and American economic growth: Essays in economic history*. Baltimore, MD: Johns Hopkins University Press.

Friedman, M. (1962). *Capitalism and freedom*. Chicago, IL: University of Chicago Press.

Galbraith, J. K. (1987). *Economics in perspective: A critical history*. Boston, MA: Houghton Mifflin.

Glamann, K. (1977). The changing patterns of trade. In E. E. Rich & C. H. Wilson (Eds.), *The Economic Organisation of Early Modern Europe: Vol. 5. Cambridge economic history of Europe* (pp. 185–289). Cambridge: Cambridge University Press.
Gudeman, S. (1978). *The demise of a rural economy: From subsistence to capitalism in a Latin American village*. London: RKP.
Hann, C., & Hart, K. (Eds.), (2010). *Market and society: The great transformation today*. Cambridge: Cambridge University Press.
Harvey, D. (2005). *A brief history of neoliberalism*. Oxford: Oxford University Press.
Herzog, L. (2013). *Inventing the market: Smith, Hegel, and political theory*. Oxford: Oxford University Press.
Hill, P. (1972). *Rural Hausa: A village and a setting*. Cambridge: Cambridge University Press.
Hirschman, A. O. (1977). *The passions and the interests: Political arguments for capitalism before its triumph*. Princeton, NJ: Princeton University Press.
Hont, I. (2015). Politics in commercial society: Jean-Jacques Rousseau and Adam Smith. In B. Kapossy & M. Sonenscher (Eds.), Cambridge, MA: Harvard University Press.
Jones, A., & Moskoff, W. (Eds.), (1991). *The great market debate in soviet economics*. London: Routledge.
Knorr-Cetina, K., & Preda, A. (Eds.), (2013). *The oxford handbook of the sociology of finance*. Oxford: Oxford University Press.
Kornai, J. (1992). *The socialist system: The political economy of communism*. Princeton, NJ: Princeton University Press.
Lange, O., & Taylor, F. M. (1938). In B. E. Lippincott (Ed.), *On the economic theory of socialism*. Minneapolis, MN: University of Minnesota Press.
Lenin, V. I. (1956). *The development of capitalism in Russia: The process of the formation of a home market for large-scale industry*. Moscow: Foreign Language Publishing House.
Lewin, M. (1985). *The making of the soviet system: Essays in the social history of interwar Russia*. New York: Pantheon.
Lie, J. (1992). The concept of mode of exchange. *American Sociological Review, 57*, 508–523.
Lie, J. (1997). Sociology of markets. *Annual Review of Sociology, 23*, 341–360.
Lie, J. (2014). The concept of mode of exchange: An auto-critique. *Korea Observer, 45*, 483–491.
MacKenzie, D. (2006). *An engine, not a camera*. Cambridge: MIT Press.
North, D. C., & Thomas, R. P. (1973). *The rise of the western world: A new economic history*. Cambridge: Cambridge University Press.
O'Hara, M. (1995). *Market microstructure theory*. New York: Wiley.
Parsons, T., & Smelser, N. J. (1956). *Economy and society: A study in the integration of economic and social theory*. New York: Free Press.
Phillipson, N. (2010). *Adam Smith*. New Haven, CT: Yale University Press.
Polanyi, K. (1957 [1944]). *The great transformation*. Boston, MA: Beacon Press.
Polanyi, K. (1971). The economy as instituted process. In G. Dalton (Ed.), *Primitive, archaic and modern economies* (pp. 139–174). Boston, MA: Beacon Press.
Rodrik, D. (2015). *Economics rules: The rights and wrongs of the dismal science*. New York: Norton.
Slater, D., & Tonkiss, F. (2001). *Market society: Markets and modern social theory*. Cambridge: Polity.
Smith, A. (1981). *An inquiry into the nature and causes of the wealth of nations*. Indianapolis, IN: Liberty Press.
Spies-Butcher, B., Paton, J., & Cahill, D. (2012). *Market society: History, theory, practice*. Cambridge: Cambridge University Press.
Thaler, R. H. (2015). *Misbehaving: The making of behavioral economics*. New York: Norton.
Ubel, P. A. (2008). *Free market madness: Why human nature is at odds with economics—and why it matters*. Cambridge: Harvard Business Review Press.
Winch, D. (1978). *Adam Smith's politics*. Cambridge: Cambridge University Press.
Wolmar, C. (2012). *The great railroads revolution: The history of trains in America*. New York: Public Affairs.

CHAPTER 3

Confucianism and Work Ethic—Introducing the ReVaMB Model

C. Baumann*,[†], H. Winzar*
*Macquarie University, Sydney, NSW, Australia
[†]Seoul National University (SNU), Seoul, South Korea

3.1 WHY THIS CHAPTER?

Confucianism is old—one of the oldest ideologies, philosophies or even religions, dating back to the Chinese philosopher Confucius (551–479 b.c.e.). So it is not quite as old as Judaism (roughly 3500 years old), but roughly the same age as Buddhism (roughly 2500 years old), and clearly older than Christianity (roughly 2000 years old) and Islam (roughly 1400 years old). It has been influential in the East Asian region for a very long time to this day, and given migration of East Asians to other parts of the world, has also influenced other cultures in the West (e.g., California in the United States or British Columbia in Canada that have large Chinese, Korean, and Vietnamese communities).

Confucianism has also changed over time, given that it tracks such a long history, with different facets even in its large country of origin, China, but also to other parts of East Asia such as Japan, Hong Kong, Korea, Singapore, Taiwan, and Vietnam. Confucianism has therefore been the focus of countless scholarly investigations in terms of culture (language, music, manners), but only recently has been spotted as a candidate to "drive" progression in East Asia and also of East Asian migrants in the West. Progression in what way?

Confucianism appears to strongly affect the way education "works," and given that students are the workforce of the future, it is also likely that Confucianism directly impacts work ethic, productivity and performance. East Asia has experienced strong economic growth beyond the West late last century, and has superseded the West in terms of educational performance, at least according to Programme for International Student Assessment (PISA). A recent study (Baumann, Hamin, & Yang, 2016) has established that pedagogical approaches such as strict discipline and a focus

on academic performance, very prominent in Confucian based East Asian education, but not so in Western countries, are significantly linked with work ethic. We pick up from that stream of research and probe the idea that indeed Confucianism may directly (and indirectly) relate, impact, form, or at least contribute, to a Confucian work ethic (CWE).

Despite the recognition that Confucian culture plays a formative role in the shaping of attitudes and behaviors, few studies have examined its influence on employee performance, for example in a service context where Confucian elements such as respect could play an important role (Tsang, 2011). He developed and refined dimensions of the well-established *Chinese Cultural Values (CCV)* (Chinese Culture Connection, 1987; Hofstede & Bond, 1988) to understand better frontline employees' attitude and behaviors towards the provision of service, possibly to reflect a CWE.

We are also very aware of the risk and frequent practice, especially among Western writers, of conflating all "Confucian" cultures into one homogenous lump. This is a particularly insidious form of the Ecological Fallacy, where all people in a group are regarded as equal to the average of a group, or to the average of a small sample of the group (Winzar, 2015). We are reminded of a comment from our friend and mentor, Professor Rosalie Tung, an esteemed scholar of International Business:

> Every invitation to write or speak about Asian management practices reminds me of a social studies text that my daughter used when she was in Grade 5 in a US mid-western school, in 1987. At the beginning of the school year, her teacher proudly announced to the parents that the students were going to learn about Asia that year. As the academic year progressed and as a dutiful mother, I helped my daughter prepare for her exam by reviewing the questions at the end of each chapter of her text. When it came to the chapter on Asia – an entire chapter was devoted to the whole of Asia – there was a question on "what are the three characteristics of Asians". My daughter had obviously studied for the exam as she rattled off her answer: "First characteristic, they are all farmers". I interjected by telling her that this was not the case and reminded her of her visits to Tokyo and Seoul. Unfazed, she went on to recite the second characteristic, "they are poor" – again, I interrupted her by recounting her experience on her trips to these two Asian capitals. She then abruptly curtailed my remarks by asking me "not to confuse her in preparing for her exam". Because the immediate priority was for her to perform well in her exam, I desisted from my attempts to correct the erroneous portrait of Asia and Asians etched in the minds of our children. This incident, however, alerted me to the dangers of lumping widely disparate countries together as a homogeneous region (Asia in this case) and, worse yet, to view them through stereotypical lenses that are grossly outdated. Similarly, the tendency to treat European countries, USA, Canada, Australia and New Zealand as a monolithic whole under the broad rubric of "Western" is equally as problematic.

Tung, 2014, p. 189

This chapter explores the "Confucianism—Work Ethic" association in more depth, starting with a generalized conceptual framework on values and behavior; a new model we label ReVaMB and will subsequently explain in detail. Each of the components of the conceptual framework are examined in light of Confucian philosophy and current understandings of work ethic, so that we can derive an elaborated conceptual framework specifically for CWE. This allows us to propose directions for further research, and identify specific problems in measurement and analysis of workplace behavior and of values research generally and in Confucianism specifically.

3.2 VALUES AND BEHAVIOR: A NEW CONCEPTUAL FRAMEWORK (ReVaMB)

In this chapter, we propose a broad model of the relationship between Values and Workplace Behavior. Consistent with Fishbein and Ajzen (1975), we propose a straightforward model where personal values drive behavior as illustrated in Fig. 3.1. Additionally, we posit that how much values drive behavior is a function of the circumstances in which individuals find themselves. Most importantly, values alone do not drive behavior, but the relative importance of competing values in different circumstances.

3.2.1 Relative Values

For almost everyone, personal values are shared. Most people agree on basic values statements on, for example, caring for children, honesty, or equity within a group. How those values are manifested as actual behavior, however, can vary greatly by how important those values are relative to other values. Among consumers in widely varying cultures—Germany, Spain, Turkey, United States, India, Korea—that there are surprisingly consistent patterns of relative importance of ethical perspectives on issues such as child labor, women's rights, product safety and recycling (Auger, Devinney, &

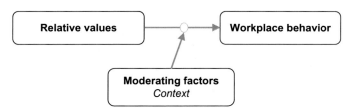

Fig. 3.1 Generalized conceptual framework: relative values and moderated behavior (ReVaMB).

Louviere, 2007). To consider values and attitudes independently of other values and attitudes loses valuable information about the trade-offs all of us must make to get by each day.

The *World Values Survey Association* (*WVS*) produces wide-ranging measures of different value perspectives from most countries in the world (World Values Survey, 2016). Example 1, illustrates one of the questions that might be regarded as a fundamental feature of Confucian philosophy: "One of my main goals in life has been to make my parents proud." The response format is a four-point Agree-Disagree scale which forces respondents to take a side on an issue. Unfortunately, it is also an issue that almost everyone agrees with: The median score for more than half of the countries surveyed was 1 (Strongly agree) and the median for the remainder was 2 (Agree). This also means that the other option (3 and 4) were practically unused. That raised serious concerns about measuring Culture, Values or Confucianism in this fashion.

Example 1: Extract from World Values Survey (Question 49)

V49. One of my main goals in life has been to make my parents proud
Strongly agree   Agree   Disagree   Strongly disagree

Other questions in the *WVS* are drawn from Schwartz (1992) like those in Example 2. These are 6-point rating scale questions asking to what extent a respondent identifies with the person described. The distribution of responses is considerably wider for such questions, but it is clear also that most respondents see themselves, or want to present themselves, as a "good person." Very rarely is there much variation in a person's assessment of himself, or herself, on questions that might compromise other questions. For example, most people would like the idea of a good material lifestyle, and most people like the idea of helping others in their community, but the accumulation of wealth and power may not easily work with the care and wellbeing of others in society. How does a person behave when the possibility of helping others conflicts with the opportunity to earn more money? Or when a business opportunity could make others worse off? When people are placed in a situation where they have to choose between potentially conflicting values then the relative importance of those values, in that particular situation, is what drives behavior.

> **Example 2: Sample Schwartz Values Questions in World Values Survey**
>
> | Very much like me | Like me | Somewhat like me | A little like me | Not like me | Not at all like me |
> |---|---|---|---|---|---|
> | 1 | 2 | 3 | 4 | 5 | 6 |
>
> **Questions:**
> V71. It is important to this person to be rich; to have a lot of money and expensive things.
> V74. It is important to this person to do something for the good of society.
> V74B. It is important for this people to help the people nearby; to care for their wellbeing
> V79. Tradition is important to this person; to follow the customs handed down by one's religion or family.

An examination of the answers to the question "One of my main goals in life has been to make my parents proud" from the most recently available *WVS* are illustrated in Fig. 3.2. We were surprised to see that average responses for many "Confucian" countries are up among the most Western countries in their level of non-agreement with what is surely one of the most basic Confucian values. What is going on? A four-point rating scale is not uncommon, and similar scales are used in all of the social sciences for measuring attitudes and stated values, albeit often 7 point scales are used that—at least—allow a larger spread than the (too) limited 4 point scale. Perhaps the question translated to a different meaning in different countries. Perhaps different cultures respond to the scale in different ways. Perhaps that too limited 4-point scale. We can't know for sure. What is not being captured in such a question, however, is the extent that "making my parents proud" is more important than, say, "making a lot of money." For example, there are many ways that parents may be proud without their children making a lot of money (such as becoming a university professor) and there may be many ways to make a lot of money that do not make your parents proud. If I strongly agree that I want to make my parents proud and also strongly agree that I want to earn a lot of money, then which is more important?

Most measures of values, and attitudes generally, are taken using normative scales. It is assumed that one respondent's rating of, say, "5" on a 6-point scale is the same as any other respondent's rating of "5." Averages of very large samples of relatively homogenous people work well enough to

38   The Political Economy of Business Ethics in East Asia

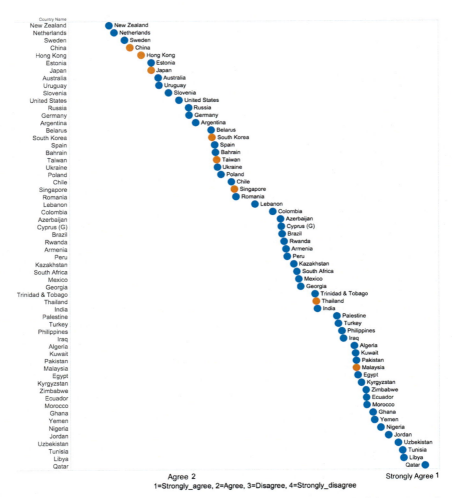

Fig. 3.2 World values survey (2016) mean responses question49. "One of the main goals in life has been to make my parents proud". Notes: Four-point rating scale: 1 = "Strongly agree," 2 = "Agree," 3 = "Disagree," 4 = "Strongly Disagree." X-axis on this graph is cut off at 2.5 because no averages appeared beyond that point.

get a score but we can't know if that score means something different from the score of another group. More importantly, normative scales are evaluated and rated on their own. Judgments are made of each concept without reference to any other concept. For example "is Toshiba a good laptop PC brand?", "is Samsung a good laptop PC brand?", "which is the better laptop PC brand: Toshiba or Samsung?" As a result, our measures of personal

values and other drivers of attitudes and behaviors fail to take account of the daily trade-offs that everyone must make when values come into conflict or when circumstances force us to choose among different motivations. Cultural values are no different, we argue, and thus propose our new framework where we allow for values to be relative (as opposed to static).

3.2.2 Workplace Behavior

It is likely that Confucianism may play a positive role in workplace behavior, especially when it comes to the provision of services (education, medical, transportation, hospitality, tourism, retailing). In a service context, employee presentation includes the frontline employees' overall demeanor as well as their capacity to provide a smooth and natural flowing service experience. Service provision is often about providing accurate service, whilst maintaining a harmonious atmosphere during the service experience. Relationalism is a key feature of Confucianism, manifested through ritualistic traditions (greetings, courteous behavior, bowing to superior, students standing up when teacher/professor enters) (Ho, 1998a). This performance of respect for others, and in our application case of CWE, for example a customer, is the result of "an awareness and empathy for the thoughts and feelings of others" (Ho, 1998b, p. 15). Such rituals are rather unique to East Asian culture and service quality, which contrasts that of Western "standards": Western notions of service reliability are oriented towards task completion and outcomes (Tsang, 2011), the Asian paradigm includes the outcome to be subject to unknown environmental influences (Chen, 2002). In East Asian culture then, frontline employees enact a sense of sincerity exemplified through physical cues in order to demonstrate benevolence as well as a wholehearted rather than calculated effort towards service.

Imrie, Cadogan, and McNaughton (2002) suggest that the Confucian element of respect reflects a customer's anticipation of a "master-servant" type relationship. Showing respect is part of the employee's role requirement. Naturally, such interpretations of Asian predisposition and culture to subservience, for example in a service setting, border on stereotyping and should be treated with caution (Yen, 2000). Meanwhile, in a Confucian setting, the emphasis is placed on employees observing the order of relationships and authority as it would be in family, education and society at large, but also in the workplace, with performance orientation geared towards pleasing superiors (Mok & Hui, 1998). We also draw from Johns, Chan, and Yeung (2003) work that employees' willingness to serve is interpreted as a personal deference to the employer.

3.2.3 Confucian Work Ethic

The basic premise of our work is that Confucianism may be related to work ethic, or more broadly, workplace behavior. The psychology and human resource management literature has long focused on work ethic and debated whether it is a matter of inertia, an emotional attachment to work or the workplace, whether it can be simply (and naively) measured as hours worked? Or is work ethic a Human Resources Management matter of turnover rate? Is work ethic a matter of going beyond what a job description formally expects of an employee, and employees go beyond for monetary reasons (bonus incentives) or fame and pride?

Perhaps one of the most often referred scholar in the field is Paula Morrow who has done early and influential research on work commitment (Morrow, 1983; Morrow & Goetz, 1988), including on its measurement (Morrow, 1993). In fact, what started early last century with Weber's proposition of a Protestant Work Ethic (PWE), was picked up again in the literature in the 1980s/90s with a rather influential review of the psychological literature on work ethic (Furnham, 1984). That review questioned the usefulness of PWE as a predictor of behavior, values and job satisfaction, arguing that researchers focused on relationships between PWE and work *per se*, rather than on leisure, economic behavior and health. Further, it was then argued that other aspects of personality traits may also play a role, and that the focus of PWE research may well have been on commitment to paid work whereas work ethic may well relate to other areas of life (volunteer work, sport, culture).

Roughly a decade after the Furnham review on the topic, a new piece emerged on the "neglected work commitment facet" (Blau & Ryan, 1997, p. 435) of work ethic. Four dimensions emerged from that angle on measuring work ethic: hard work, nonleisure, independence, and asceticism (i.e., severe self-discipline), with those dimensions impacting subsequent work ethic research.

Another decade later a piece emerged on the "meaning and measurement of work ethic," suggesting that the construct may be multidimensional (Miller, Woehr, & Hudspeth, 2002). A review of previous work ethic measures (see Table 3.1 in that manuscript) provides a useful overview of previous measurement studies, ranging from 1961 to 1984, and pointing towards a strong focus on PWE paradigms (4 out of 7 studies focused on that Protestant theme). That study itself departed from the idea of a PWE, however, but instead proposed seven dimensions to capture simply work ethic without the Protestant connotation: self-reliance, morality/ethics, leisure, hard work, centrality of work, wasted time, and delay of gratification., all of which arguably are consistent with might be seen as a CWE.

Table 3.1 Confucian work ethic

Antecedents	Value system	Moderating factors

Inter-generational influences
Parenting
Education
• Focus on
  • Performance
  • Discipline
  • Respect
  • Value of education
Harmony in human relationships
	Confucian work ethic
	• Internal motivation
	• Drive to perform
	• Drive to compete
	• Follow instructions
	• Accuracy
	• Willingness to serve
	• Appearance standards
	• Politeness
	• Punctuality
	• Frugality
		Context
		• Social norms
		• Organizational type
		• Organization size
		• Level of bureaucracy
		• Local ownership vis-à-vis Foreign ownership
		• Government vis-à-vis private sector
		• In-group vis-à-vis Out-group

Adapted from Table 1: Evolution of institutional approach to education in Baumann, C., Hamin, H., & Yang, S. J. (2016). Work ethic formed by pedagogical approach: Evolution of institutional approach to education and competitiveness. *Asia Pacific Business Review*, 1–21, p. 8.

The most recent study considered for our study at hand is also closest to our paradigm, that is, that culture may be an important driver of how people are educated (parents, family, school, university) and that it turn drives their work ethic with subsequent performance. Baumann and his colleagues (Baumann, Hamin, & Yang, 2016) measured work ethic on a single item construct of "I enjoy working hard." Pedagogical approaches prominent in East Asia such as strict discipline and a focus on academic performance were significantly associated with work ethic in Asia, but not in Western countries. This also means that there is evidence to suggest that the Confucian way of educating the next generation may well be linked with higher levels of work ethic, with the observed strong performance in education, sport, culture and economic progression in East Asia.

A recent study (Pogson, Cober, Doverspike, & Rogers, 2003) picked up the work ethic dimensions developed by Miller, Woehr, and Hudspeth (2002) and probed them for differences across three career stages: trial stage, stabilization stage, and maintenance stage. As expected, different work ethic components are prominent at various career stages, for example, employees at the trial stage focus on hard work, whereas the ones at the maintenance stage emphasize leisure dimensions. Similarly Weng and colleagues' work on career growth and organizational commitment (Weng, McElroy, Morrow, & Liu, 2010) point to the different behaviors of individuals depending on their perceived success and place within an organization. This leads us to consider the moderating role of the context in which values are allowed to become manifest.

We should be careful here to note that Work Ethic and Commitment are very different things, although they may be correlated within an organization. Generally Commitment is seen as an emotional and behavioral attachment to an organization. But frequently we see Commitment at two levels; commitment to a profession and commitment to an organization. Doctors and nurses, for example, generally have a very strong commitment to the profession of medicine, regardless of their experience of the bureaucracy or hospital setting where they might work. Similar observations can be made of academics, pilots, teachers, artists, and athletes.

Performance on a broader scale, and work ethic may not be dissimilar, has recently been established to be driven by competitive attitude, willingness to serve and speed for the Asian workforce (Baumann, Hamin, Tung, & Hoadley, 2016). From that research, three country clusters emerged: (a) emerging economies in Asia (Indonesia, India) where the aforementioned factors powerfully explained performance; (b) "Confucian orbit countries" (China, Japan, Korea) where the factors explained 81–93%; (c) highly developed Western countries (United States, United Kingdom, Germany) where the same factors accounted for 20–29% (Baumann, Hamin, Tung, et al., 2016). We have incorporated these three dimensions in our new framework under Workplace Behavior, or specifically applied under CWE, as Drive to compete, Willingness to serve, and speed of work.

3.3 THE ReVaMB MODEL APPLIED TO CONFUCIANISM

Taking the generalized ReVaMB model and applying the CWE framework suggested by Baumann, Hamin, and Yang (2016), we offer the applied model illustrated in Fig. 3.3. We can see that this application maintains the same structure as the generalized model, with the addition of antecedent factors. This application specifically identifies key Confucian values and hypothesized workplace behaviors plus specific key moderating factors.

3.3.1 Antecedent Factors

A complete model of the relationship between values and behavior should acknowledge the origins of those values. We do not intend to offer a complete description of the infinite combinations of nature and nurture that produce each human's perspective of the world, but it is worth highlighting some contributions to our understanding of the development of Confucian values (or not).

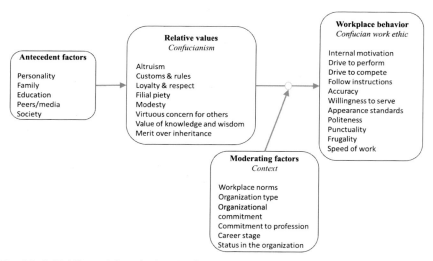

Fig. 3.3 ReVaMB model applied to Confucianism.

3.3.1.1 Society

Low- and High-context Cultural Dimensions proposed by Hall (1989) support the notion introduced in his influential Low- and High-context Cultural Dimensions Model some quarter century ago, which suggests that cultural experiences shape the beliefs and attitudes and guide the behavior of people, in line with our new ReVaMB model where we link value to behavior. Cultural values, of course, vary from one country to another, (and in many ways, from ethnicity to ethnicity) and that in turn develops nation (or culture) specific competencies (Tsang, 2011). That theory is captured in Cultural Difference Theory (Banks, 1993; Cole & Bruner, 1971) that argues that all cultures differ from one another and have varying assets, or "cultural capital" (Bourdieu, 1986; Bourdieu & Wacquant, 1992).

As captured by the term Confucian Orbit by Baumann and colleagues (2016a), East Asia has been classified as a group of nations/cultures influenced by a long tradition of Confucian teachings and principles, having influenced individual values and norms (Warner & Rowley, 2010). Confucian culture also drives a nation's institutional development, for example in the case of East Asian academic success with their Confucian approach to pedagogy (Marginson, 2010), and beyond institutional theory, business management practices (Lim Leung & Bozionelos, 2004; Zhu & Warner, 2000). Confucianism with related CWE also explains, at least in part, the dimensions of individual performance and competitiveness at the micro-level

(Baumann, Tung, & Hamin, 2012; Baumann & Winzar, 2016) and to understand consumer behavior (Monkhouse, Barnes, & Hanh Pham, 2013).

3.3.1.2 Personality

Personality refers to individuals' characteristic patterns of thought, emotion, and behavior, together with the psychological mechanisms—hidden or not—behind those patterns (Funder, 2015, p. 7). Patterns of thought affect the way a person perceives the world and any situations she finds herself, (or he himself) which, in turn, affect behavior in those situations. Personality characteristics seem to relate to varying levels of success within an organization across different cultural settings. For example, Lim Leung and Bozionelos (2004) tested the association between the "five-factor model" of personality (Extraversion, Conscientiousness, Agreeableness, Emotional stability, and Openness) and the prototypical image of the "Effective Leader" among Hong Kong Chinese individuals. Effective leaders were seen to have high levels of extraversion, conscientiousness, agreeableness, emotional stability and openness. Extroverted leaders were expected in Western cultures, but it was also the most cited expectation within this Confucian cohort. And that notion also was linked to the features of Transformational Leadership, perhaps also a key feature of a Confucian education that aspires to make the youth better on all dimensions, not just academically, but including character building. The findings imply that most of the conclusions on the relationship between personality traits and leader emergence drawn from Anglo-Saxon samples are generalizable in Confucian societies.

Using a somewhat different theoretical perspective on personality, King and colleagues concluded that "Competitiveness is not that bad," especially not for the Confucian-driven East Asian students. They found for Chinese students, both trait competitiveness and the adoption of performance goals are related to positive performance outcomes, the same as for American students (King, McInerney, & Watkins, 2012).

3.3.1.3 Life Experiences

Like personality, life experiences are those aspects of the individual that help to create values and perceptions. Parenting styles, peers, and formal education all combine to create very different individuals (Berger, 2014).

3.3.2 Moderating Factors

3.3.2.1 Context

Beyond Hall's (1989) invaluable contribution to our understanding of High-context and Low-context cultures, we can consider more tangible contextual environments that affect employees' behavior and the

relationship between Confucian values and Work Ethic. Here we refer to Context as simply the physical and social environment that an employee may find himself in the workplace. Observable contexts might include, but are not limited to, Organization type, Social norms within the organization, and Career stage of the employee,

3.3.2.2 Organization Type

Organization type might be measured in terms of ownership or management structure.

Family-Owned/ Employee

The obligations and expectations within a family, for most people, create their own incentives for selflessness and commitment to work. Manager-employees and line-employees create opportunities for moral hazard (Eisenhardt, 1989; Mirrlees, 1976), which is "any situation in which one person makes the decision about how much risk to take, while someone else bears the cost if things go badly" (Krugman, 2008).

Indigenous/Foreign-Multinational

Implicit in this suggested moderator is the notion that some employees may have greater loyalties to companies based in their own countries, and less loyalty to foreign-owned companies. Work ethic variation may differ among foreign employees and domestic employees also (Monagahan, 2014).

3.3.2.3 Social Norms Within the Organization

Organizations develop their own culture—their own way of doing things, modes of recognition, status symbols and so on. With these are the nature of communications structure within an organization and the extent that the organizational culture promotes internal competition or cooperation.

Interpersonal Influences

The relationships that employees have with their co-workers clearly has an impact on how they approach their work. Specifically, we might speculate that when the behavior of others violates the values of a person, then that person's willingness to engage with the others is likely to be compromised.

Competitive/Cooperative

Some people thrive on a daily effort to get ahead of their peers, but the majority of us prefer to not have to "fight multiple battles" just to get our jobs done. And a cooperative and supportive environment is preferred by both men and women in their preferences for employers (Catanzaro, Moore, & Marshall, 2010).

3.3.2.4 Career Stage

Employees can be seen to move through different stages in their careers, including: Trial, Stabilization, and Maintenance (Super, 1957). While loosely related to age and maturity, each stage involves different personal motivations and self-perceptions of capabilities, prospects, and role in the world. Consider our earlier example from Pogson, Cober, Doverspike, and Rogers (2003) who examined differences in work ethic across career stages. Participants in the trial stage scored significantly higher on the hard work and delay of gratification dimensions, but participants in the stabilization and maintenance stages scored higher on the morality, wasted time, and leisure dimensions. The results provide evidence of the importance of studying work ethic across the lifespan and of the multidimensional nature of the work ethic construct (Pogson et al., 2003).

3.4 CONFUCIANISM IN THE WORKPLACE

It has been argued that Korean workers' voluntary participation in industrial work coupled with harmony in the workplace were two of the most vital factors in South Korea's notable economic success during the 1960s and 1970s, both to Confucianism with an associate CWE. That in turn, at the time, created a new ideology of work and entrepreneurship and combined with nationalism lead to pro-growth Confucian precepts (Kim & Park, 2003). CWE emphasizes the importance of hard work, loyalty and dedication, frugality, and a love of learning (Rarick, 2007).

> The philosophical foundations of Confucianism have created a certain work ethic in China and East Asia that is not too far removed from the Protestant ethic proposed by Weber. The Confucian Work Ethic consists of a belief in the value of hard work, loyalty to the organization, thrift, dedication, social harmony, a love of education and wisdom, and a concern for social propriety. The elements of the Confucian Work Ethic all have positive aspects for economic development. The elements also have positive aspects for societal development. Confucius recognized that in order to build a nation, certain sacrifices would have to be made by the individual. Personal sacrifice in order to advance the interests of the nation is found in all Confucian societies, including China. When one compares the Protestant Work Ethic with the principles espoused by Confucius, it becomes obvious that there are really more similarities than differences. Both work ethics place an emphasis on hard work and thrift. In both approaches, employees are expected to achieve a form of self-fulfilment, and perhaps spiritual fulfilment as well through dedication and devotion to work. Rather than concentrating on spiritual salvation, adherents are required to focus on achievement in this life. Confucius de-emphasized the importance of paying respect to the spirits and, not unlike Protestantism, preached

achievement in this life. The difference between the Confucian and Protestant work ethics is mainly in the focus on individual or group achievement. Whereas the Protestant Work Ethic looks at the individual as the appropriate unit of analysis, the Confucian Work Ethic places a value on group achievement and social harmony. Achievement is more group-focused in Confucian societies and economic failure is seen as having more widespread societal consequences. The Confucian Work Ethic maintains a social interconnection that it not commonly found in Western cultures. Many times these interconnections are family based, especially in Chinese entrepreneurial culture.

(Rarick, 2007, p. 26)

Fang (2014) has suggested several unique strategies that Confucian executives use in business and with each other, as shown in Table 3.2. We can see that on the face of it, these modes of behavior may seem contradictory or countering other strategies. But they are quite consistent when taken in context.

These strategies may appear to counteract each other. For example, can one "Compromise" and "Strive for total victory" at the same time? Perhaps, if comprise is a means to the goal of total victory at a future time (Patience). Alternatively, in different environments different goals, and different modes for achieving them, may take priority. Fang goes on to explain:

East Asians, who have no indigenous religion akin to Judaism and Christianity, consider deception a neutral term—it is amoral and acceptable if it results in a greater good. From the East Asian perspective, "the greater good" embraces the wellbeing of the nation-state, the clan (the geographic region from which a person's ancestors came), the extended family, the nuclear family, the corporation (employer), and the self. Their order of importance, however, varies among East Asian countries.

Table 3.2 Confucian competitive strategies
1. The importance of strategies
2. Transforming an adversary's strength into weakness
3. Engaging in deception to gain a strategic advantage
4. Understanding contradictions and using them to gain an advantage
5. Compromising
6. Striving for total victory
7. Taking advantage of an adversary's or competitor's misfortune
8. Flexibility
9. Gathering intelligence and information
10. Grasping the interdependent relationship of situations
11. Patience
12. Avoiding strong emotions

Fang, 2014, p. 78.

In Japan, for example, the nation-state usually tops the hierarchy. This explains the willingness of World War II kamikaze pilots to sacrifice their lives for the perceived good of their country. In China, Hong Kong, and Taiwan, the family is usually considered paramount. And a hierarchy exists within the family. For example, filial piety to parents is considered most important. Next comes obligations to blood brothers and "sworn" brothers, who are not related by birth but take a solemn oath of brotherhood for life.

(Fang, 2014, p. 97)

At the end of the day, culture drives performance and competitiveness, or in our exemplar in Fig. 3.3, Confucianism drives a CWE, essentially the "flow" of Table 3.1. We also offer specific operationalizations of the constructs we have in our model.

3.5 CONCLUSION

The purpose of our chapter was to explore the association between Confucianism and work ethic. Initially, we propose a generalized conceptual framework of the relationship between values and behavior where situational circumstances moderate that association. That model is applicable to our Confucianism and work ethic debate, yet it is also applicable beyond that research challenge. The new way of thinking is that values are relative when they impact workplace behavior, again, mediated by the situation. In other words, we argue that previous conceptualization and measurements of culture may have overlooked two important factors: (a) that values are likely to be indeed relative as opposed to normative, and (b) that how values associates with (workplace, and other) behavior may well be mediated by specific situations.

We apply our generalized conceptual framework to the case of Confucianism, resulting in an elaborated conceptual model for Confucianism. Relative values represent Confucianism that in turn impact workplace behavior, or CWE specifically in this application. Moderating factors are contextual, such as workplace norms or organization type.

3.6 IMPLICATIONS AND FUTURE RESEARCH

This chapter is a brief summary of our considerations of the way Confucianism affects Work Ethic. Clearly some are hypotheses and much is open to verification and further research. There are implications here for theory, comparative evaluation and current practice.

3.6.1 Implications for Theory
3.6.1.1 Is Work Ethic a Cultural Issue Anyway?
This chapter has taken CWE as a template to outline a broader theoretical perspective of the relationship between core values and workplace behavior. We could also raise similar questions about other philosophical and religious values perspectives. We have noted, for example, that actual behavior of Confucian workers is only marginally different from those of Western managers with respect "PWE," and observed differences could just as easily be explained without recourse to Confucian values. Similarly, should we be surprised that studies of Sufi and Islamic professional managers appeared to display higher levels of PWE than their Protestant counterparts (Arslan, 2000; Owoyemi, 2012).

At a more philosophical level, perhaps we should consider whether the extent that we are simply buying into a propaganda statement about the implicitly "good" nature of a work ethic. What should we expect of workers who may see little opportunity for growth or purpose in their employment? We are reminded of comments from social theorist, Zygmunt Bauman:

> *Whenever you hear people talking about ethics, you should be pretty sure that someone somewhere is dissatisfied with the way some other people behave and would rather have them behaving differently. Hardly ever has this advise made more sense than in the case of the work ethic.*
>
> *Since it erupted into the European consciousness in the early stages of industrialization and it's many avatars throughout the twisted itinerary of modernity and 'modernisation' the work ethic served politicians, philosophers and preachers alike as a clarion call to, or excuse for, attempts to uproot, by hook or by crook, the popular habit which they saw as the prime obstacle to the new brave world intended to build: the allegedly widespread inclination to avoid, if one could, the ostensible blessings of factory employment, and to resist docile submission to the rhythm of life set by the foreman, the clock and the machine.*
>
> **(Bauman, 2005, p. 6)**

3.6.2 Implications for Values/Behavior Research
Our generalized conceptual framework of relationship between values and behavior should form the basis for future research on international business, culture and cross cultural studies, and other research where values come into play. Values are derived/based on a variety of ideologies, religions and philosophies, meanwhile we apply our new framework to Confucianism. We offer a detailed operationalization of our framework to

Confucianism and a CWE, and that should form a basis for further testing on East Asian culture. In addition, future researchers could take our framework as a foundation to probe other ideologies, religions and philosophies and their association with (workplace) behavior, moderated by situational circumstances.

Challenges ahead appear to be on specific measurements of the constructs and variables we suggest. As often if not always, some variables "sit on the fence," that is, they could be attitudinal or behavioral. In the case of Confucianism, our elaborated model provides an example that may serve as a role model on how to operationalize our framework, yet some variables such as modesty, for example, could quite possibly be modeled as part of relative values (i.e., part of Confucianism) or then as workplace behavior (or CWE). Future research is invited to probe the specific inclusion of the suggested variables more clearly in their specific roles in the framework. We also propose antecedent factors for relative values, arguing that they are formed by personality, family, education, peers/media and society at large, and future research should also explore the relative importance of these antecedents in forming (relative) values, since they may well—in turn—impact behavior.

3.6.3 Implications for Policy and Practice

Our work also has implications for policy makers, or practice in terms of pedagogy, education and of course work place management, human resource management. Integrating our framework's components into policy making should prove useful, especially since the proposed associations between relative values and behavior may have been previously overlooked when it comes to policy on education and workplace management. The antecedents we propose that drive and form relative values need to be better understood and then also better integrated into education and school policy, for instance. The pedagogical approach in schools and at universities is suggested to directly impact values such as customs, rules, virtuous concern for others, value of a knowledge and wisdom. If such values are nurtured (or not) in education and child rearing, then this will also directly impact (workplace) behavior. In other words, education drives performance at the micro level, and as we have suggested in earlier work, also at the macro level where we have demonstrated how education drives competitiveness (Baumann & Winzar, 2016). This also means that our model may well have direct implications for nation building and economic welfare.

APPENDIX

In this appendix, we briefly review the traditional, normative, approach to item measurement and propose a straightforward adaptation designed to discover the relative importance of values statements, thus constructing an ipsative scale from which real context-moderated behavioral decisions are made. Ipsative, from Latin "of the self," means that comparisons are only appropriate within the one person. An ipsative measure shows that an object (or value) is more important than another object for this person. Both objects may be highly desirable, or not very important, but when a choice must be made then one is chosen. In different circumstances the relative importance of objects may change. For example, working within a family we might expect more cooperation and helping than with an "outgroup."

Here we demonstrate how the normative constructs used by more traditional researchers can be reframed as ipsative scales to extract measures of relative values.

Measurement of Relative Values

We suggest a measurement based on an ipsative perspective, where values are presented in a hierarchy similar to the original Rokeach Values Survey (RVS) (Rokeach, 1973). In the RVS, respondents rank ordered as many as 18 instrumental values (modes of behavior) and 18 terminal values (life goals). (18! = 6.402373705728E+15 permutations, or more than 6.4 million millions). A smaller number of options reduces this number considerably—eight value statements gives 40,320 rank-ordered permutations. Alternatively, adaptations of random-utility theory (Thurstone, 1927) can give very usable and familiar measures in a straightforward interval scale. With this approach, eight value statements can provide fully usable data with just simple 14 choice tasks from each respondent. Our relative values measurement approach draws from recent advances in choice modeling, using Best-Worst scaling (Flynn, Louviere, Peters, & Coast, 2007). We ask respondents to look at a subset of value statements, and choose the single most important, and the single least important, in the current circumstances.

Confucianism

Measures of CWE have been operationalized as the same thing as Confucian Dynamism as defined by Hofstede and Bond (1988). For example, Lim

(2003) adapted a scale developed by Robertson and Hoffman (2000), both of whom used CWE and Confucian Dynamism as interchangeable constructs.

Confucian Dynamism (Robertson & Hoffman, 2000)
1. Managers must be persistent to accomplish objectives.
2. There is a hierarchy to on-the-job relationships and it should be observed.
3. A good manager knows how to economize.
4. It is important to have a conscience in business.
5. Personal stability is not critical to success in business.
6. Respect for tradition hampers performance.
7. The exchange of favors and gifts is not necessary to excel.
8. Upholding one's personal image makes little difference in goal achievement.

Similarly, Leong, Huang, and Mak (2014) measured CWE as a two-dimensional construct: Confucian diligence and harmony were operationalized using the Industry scale (five items) and Civic-Harmony scale (nine items) from the Singaporean Chinese Value survey (Chang, Wong, & Koh, 2003), which was slightly modified from the Chinese Value Survey (Chinese_Culture_Connection, 1987). Participants reported how important each value was to themselves on a 9-point Likert-type scale ranging from "of no importance at all" to "of supreme importance."

To create relative values from the by Robertson and Hoffman (2000) statements we make use of a Balanced Incomplete Block (BIB) design (Batsell & Louviere, 1991; Fischer & Yates, 1949) with eight objects corresponding with the eight values statements (Table 3.3).

Each numbered item in the list of CWE statements is placed in the tasks matrix, and respondents are asked to look at each task and select the one statement that is most important, and the one statement that is least important in the current circumstances, as shown in Examples 3, 4, and 5. Note that when all 14 tasks are completed then each statement has been evaluated seven times, and compared with each other statement three times. With this BIB design there are seven opportunities for a statement to be most important and seven opportunities to be least important. The simple calculation of frequency of Most minus frequency of Least results in a scoring scheme where all eight statements are given a score ranging from −7 to +7. The scoring scheme allows for ties (indifference) among statements, and skewed preference distributions.

Table 3.3 Balanced incomplete block design—8 objects, evaluated 7 times, all pairs evaluated 3 times in 14 tasks

Task_1	Task_2	Task_3	Task_4	Task_5	Task_6	Task_7	Task_8	Task_9	Task_10	Task_11	Task_12	Task_13	Task_14
8	1	8	2	8	3	8	4	8	5	8	6	8	7
2	4	3	5	4	6	5	7	6	1	7	2	1	3
3	7	4	1	5	2	6	3	7	4	1	5	2	6
5	6	6	7	7	1	1	2	2	3	3	4	4	5

Example 3: Best-Worst Scaling Task#1

Most important   **Least important**

Upholding one's personal image makes little difference in goal achievement

There is a hierarchy to on-the-job relationships and it should be observed

A good manager knows how to economize

Personal stability is not critical to success in business

Example 4: Best-Worst Scaling Task#2

Most important   **Least important**

Managers must be persistent to accomplish objectives

It is important to have a conscience in business

The exchange of favors and gifts is not necessary to excel

Respect for tradition hampers performance

Example 5: Best-Worst Scaling Task#3

Most important   **Least important**

Upholding one's personal image makes little difference in goal achievement

A good manager knows how to economize

It is important to have a conscience in business

Respect for tradition hampers performance

Confucian Values (Monkhouse, Barnes, & Hanh Pham, 2013)

Relative measures also may be constructed from a subset of a much larger set of value statements. The Confucian Values scale used by Monkhouse et al. (2013) comprises five dimensions each with five items measured on a 1–7 rating scale. Our recommendation is to take one core statement, or

combined statement, from each dimension and then make paired comparisons, or apply a 5-statement BIB to the list.

Face Saving
1. I am concerned with not bringing shame to myself.
2. I am concerned with not bringing shame to others.
3. I pay a lot of attention to how others see me.
4. I am concerned with protecting the pride of my family.
5. I feel ashamed if I lose my face.

Humility
1. I avoid singing my own praises.
2. I try not to openly talk about my accomplishments.
3. I like to draw others' attention to my accomplishments.
4. Being boastful is a sign of weakness and insecurity.
5. I only tell others about my achievements when I am asked to.

Group Orientation
1. I recognize and respect social expectations, norms, and practices.
2. When I am uncertain how to act in a social situation, I try to do the same as what others do.
3. I usually make decisions without listening to others.
4. When I buy the same things my friends buy, I feel closer to them.
5. If there is a conflict between my interest and my family's interest, I will put priority on mine.

Hierarchy
1. I am happy if people look up to me.
1. We have a vertical order in the society that we should respect.
2. A person with high personal achievements is considered to have high social standing.
3. Wealth and power are becoming important determinants of social status.

Reciprocity
1. The practice of "give and take" of favors is an important part of social relationships.
2. I feel a sense of obligation to a person for doing me a favor.
3. It is bad manners not to return favors.
4. When I receive a big favor, I try to go an extra mile to do something nice in return.
5. When I buy a gift to say thank you to someone, I try my best to make sure the person will appreciate it.

Work Ethic

The Multidimensional Work Ethic Profile (MWEP) (Miller et al., 2002) is a 65-item inventory that measures seven conceptually and empirically distinct facets of the work ethic construct (Table 3.4). A series of six studies, using both student and nonstudent samples, examined the psychometric properties of the MWEP (Miller et al., 2002). Again, as for the previous list, a subset of seven core work-ethic statement items provides the basis for a measure of the relative value of each statement. Respondents are asked to indicate which statement is "most like me" and which statement is "Least like me."

Table 3.4 MWEP dimensions, definitions, and sample items

Dimension	Definition	Sample items
Centrality of work	Belief in work for work's sake and the importance of work	Even if I inherited a great deal of money, I would continue to work somewhere
		It is very important for me to always be able to work
		I feel content when I have spent the day working
Self-reliance	Striving for independence in one's daily work	I strive to be self-reliant
		Self-reliance is the key to being successful
		One must avoid dependence on other persons whenever possible
Hard work	Belief in the virtues of hard work	If you work hard you will succeed
		By simply working hard enough, one can achieve their goals
		Hard work makes one a better person
Leisure	Proleisure attitudes and beliefs in the importance of nonwork activities	People should have more leisure time to spend in relaxation
		The job that provides the most leisure time is the job for me
		Life would be more meaningful if we had more leisure time
Morality/ethics	Believing in a just and moral existence	People should be fair in their dealings with others
		It is never appropriate to take something that does not belong to you
		It is important to treat others as you would like to be treated

Table 3.4 MWEP dimensions, definitions, and sample items—cont'd

Dimension	Definition	Sample items
Delay of gratification	Orientation toward the future; the postponement of rewards	The best things in life are those you have to wait for If I want to buy something, I always wait until I can afford it A distant reward is usually more satisfying than an immediate one
Wasted time	Attitudes and beliefs reflecting active and productive use of time	I try to plan out my workday so as not to waste time Time should not be wasted, it should be used efficiently I constantly look for ways to productively use my time

Adapted from Miller, M. J., Woehr, D. J., & Hudspeth, N. (2002). The meaning and measurement of work ethic: Construction and initial validation of a multidimensional inventory. *Journal of Vocational Behavior*, 60(3), 451–489, p. 474.

REFERENCES

Arslan, M. (2000). A cross-cultural comparison of British and Turkish managers in terms of Protestant work ethic characteristics. *Business Ethics: A European Review*, 9(1), 13–19. http://dx.doi.org/10.1111/1467-8608.00165.

Auger, P., Devinney, T. M., & Louviere, J. J. (2007). Using best–worst scaling methodology to investigate consumer ethical beliefs across countries. *Journal of Business Ethics*, 70(3), 299–326.

Banks, J. A. (1993). Multicultural education: Historical development, dimensions, and practice. *Review of Research in Education*, 19, 3–49.

Batsell, R. R., & Louviere, J. J. (1991). Experimental analysis of choice. *Marketing Letters*, 2(3), 199–214.

Bauman, Z. (2005). *Work, consumerism and the new poor* (2nd ed.). Maidenhead: McGraw-Hill Education.

Baumann, C., Hamin, H., Tung, R. L., & Hoadley, S. (2016a). Competitiveness and workforce performance: Asia vis-à-vis the "West". *International Journal of Contemporary Hospitality Management*, 28(11) (forthcoming).

Baumann, C., Hamin, H., & Yang, S. J. (2016b). Work ethic formed by pedagogical approach: Evolution of institutional approach to education and competitiveness. *Asia Pacific Business Review*, 1–21. http://dx.doi.org/10.1080/13602381.2015.1129767.

Baumann, C., Tung, R. L., & Hamin, H. (2012). Jade will never become a work of art without being carved: Western versus Chinese attitudes toward discipline in education and society. *Virginia Review of Asian Studies*, 10(1), 1–17.

Baumann, C., & Winzar, H. (2016). The role of secondary education in explaining competitiveness. *Asia Pacific Journal of Education*, 36(1), 13–30.

Berger, K. S. (2014). *The developing person through the lifespan*. Worth Publishers; New York, NY.

Blau, G., & Ryan, J. (1997). On measuring work ethic: A neglected work commitment facet. *Journal of Vocational Behavior*, 51(3), 435–448. http://dx.doi.org/10.1006/jvbe.1996.1568.

Bourdieu, P. (1986). *The forms of capital Handbook of theory and research for the sociology of education* (pp. 241–258). New York: Greenwood.

Bourdieu, P., & Wacquant, L. J. (1992). *An invitation to reflexive sociology*. Chicago, IL: University of Chicago Press.

Catanzaro, D., Moore, H., & Marshall, T. R. (2010). The impact of organizational culture on attraction and recruitment of job applicants. *Journal of Business and Psychology, 25*(4), 649–662.

Chang, W. C., Wong, W. K., & Koh, J. B. K. (2003). Chinese values in Singapore: Traditional and modern. *Asian Journal of Social Psychology, 6*(1), 5–29. http://dx.doi.org/10.1111/1467-839X.t01-1-00007.

Chen, M.-J. (2002). Transcending paradox: The Chinese "middle way" perspective. *Asia Pacific Journal of Management, 19*(2–3), 179–199.

Chinese Culture Connection. (1987). Chinese values and the search for culture-free dimensions of culture. *Journal of Cross-Cultural Psychology, 18*(2), 143–164. http://dx.doi.org/10.1177/0022002187018002002.

Cole, M., & Bruner, J. S. (1971). Cultural differences and inferences about psychological processes. *American Psychologist, 26*(10), 867–876. http://dx.doi.org/10.1037/h0032240.

Eisenhardt, K. M. (1989). Agency theory: An assessment and review. *Academy of Management Review, 14*(1), 57–74.

Fang, T. (2014). Understanding Chinese culture and communication: The yin yang approach. In B. Gehrke & M.-T. Claes (Eds.), *Global leadership practices: A cross-cultural management perspective* (pp. 171–187). Houndmills: Palgrave Macmillan.

Fischer, R. A., & Yates, F. (1949). *Statistical tables for biological, agricultural and medical research*. New York: Hafner.

Fishbein, M., & Ajzen, I. (1975). *Belief, attitude, intention, and behavior: An introduction to theory and research*. Reading, MA: Addison-Wesley.

Flynn, T. N., Louviere, J. J., Peters, T. J., & Coast, J. (2007). Best–worst scaling: What it can do for health care research and how to do it. *Journal of Health Economics, 26*(1), 171–189. http://dx.doi.org/10.1016/j.jhealeco.2006.04.002.

Funder, D. C. (2015). *The personality puzzle* (7th ed.). New York: WW Norton & Company.

Furnham, A. (1984). The protestant work ethic: A review of the psychological literature. *European Journal of Social Psychology, 14*(1), 87–104. http://dx.doi.org/10.1002/ejsp.2420140108.

Hall, E. T. (1989). *Beyond culture*. Anchor Press; Garden City, NY.

Ho, D. Y. (1998a). Indigenous psychologies Asian perspectives. *Journal of Cross-Cultural Psychology, 29*(1), 88–103.

Ho, D. Y. (1998b). Interpersonal relationships and relationship dominance: An analysis based on methodological relationism. *Asian Journal of Social Psychology, 1*(1), 1–16.

Hofstede, G., & Bond, M. H. (1988). The Confucius connection: From cultural roots to economic growth. *Organizational Dynamics, 16*(4), 5–21. http://dx.doi.org/10.1016/0090-2616(88)90009-5.

Imrie, B. C., Cadogan, J. W., & McNaughton, R. (2002). The service quality construct on a global stage. *Managing Service Quality: An International Journal, 12*(1), 10–18.

Johns, N., Chan, A., & Yeung, H. (2003). The impact of Chinese culture on service predisposition. *The Service Industries Journal, 23*(5), 107–122.

Kim, A. E., & Park, G.-S. (2003). Nationalism, Confucianism, work ethic and industrialization in South Korea. *Journal of Contemporary Asia, 33*(1), 37–49. http://dx.doi.org/10.1080/00472330380000041.

King, R. B., McInerney, D. M., & Watkins, D. A. (2012). Competitiveness is not that bad… at least in the East: Testing the hierarchical model of achievement motivation in the Asian setting. *International Journal of Intercultural Relations, 36*(3), 446–457. http://dx.doi.org/10.1016/j.ijintrel.2011.10.003.

Krugman, P. (2008). *The return of depression economics and the crisis of 2008*. London: Allen Lane.

Leong, F. T. L., Huang, J. L., & Mak, S. (2014). Protestant work ethic, Confucian values, and work-related attitudes in Singapore. *Journal of Career Assessment*, *22*(2), 304–316. http://dx.doi.org/10.1177/1069072713493985.

Lim, V. K. G. (2003). Money matters: An empirical investigation of money, face and Confucian work ethic. *Personality and Individual Differences*, *35*(4), 953–970. http://dx.doi.org/10.1016/S0191-8869(02)00311-2.

Lim Leung, S., & Bozionelos, N. (2004). Five-factor model traits and the prototypical image of the effective leader in the Confucian culture. *Employee Relations*, *26*(1), 62–71.

Marginson, S. (2010). Higher education in East Asia and Singapore: Rise of the Confucian Model. *Higher Education*, *61*(5), 587–611. http://dx.doi.org/10.1007/s10734-010-9384-9.

Miller, M. J., Woehr, D. J., & Hudspeth, N. (2002). The meaning and measurement of work ethic: Construction and initial validation of a multidimensional inventory. *Journal of Vocational Behavior*, *60*(3), 451–489. http://dx.doi.org/10.1006/jvbe.2001.1838.

Mirrlees, J. A. (1976). The optimal structure of incentives and authority within an organization. *The Bell Journal of Economics*, 105–131.

Mok, H. M., & Hui, Y. (1998). Underpricing and aftermarket performance of IPOs in Shanghai, China. *Pacific-Basin Finance Journal*, *6*(5), 453–474.

Monagahan, A. (2014). British companies struggle to find domestic workers with right skills. *The Guardian*. Retrieved from http://www.theguardian.com/business/2014/nov/23/bcc-companies-struggle-uk-workers-eu-migrants.

Monkhouse, L. L., Barnes, B. R., & Hanh Pham, T. S. (2013). Measuring Confucian values among East Asian consumers: A four country study. *Asia Pacific Business Review*, *19*(3), 320–336. http://dx.doi.org/10.1080/13602381.2012.732388.

Morrow, P. C. (1983). Concept redundancy in organizational research: The case of work commitment. *Academy of Management Review*, *8*(3), 486–500.

Morrow, P. C. (1993). *The theory and measurement of work commitment*. Greenwich, CT: Jai Press.

Morrow, P. C., & Goetz, J. F. (1988). Professionalism as a form of work commitment. *Journal of Vocational Behavior*, *32*(1), 92–111.

Owoyemi, M. Y. (2012). The concept of Islamic work ethic: An analysis of some salient points in the prophetic tradition. *International Journal of Business and Social Science*, *3*(20), 116–123.

Pogson, C. E., Cober, A. B., Doverspike, D., & Rogers, J. R. (2003). Differences in self-reported work ethic across three career stages. *Journal of Vocational Behavior*, *62*(1), 189–201. http://dx.doi.org/10.1016/S0001-8791(02)00044-1.

Rarick, C. A. (2007). Confucius on management: Understanding Chinese cultural values and managerial practices. *Journal of International Management Studies*, *2*(2), 22–28.

Robertson, C. J., & Hoffman, J. J. (2000). How different are we? An investigation of Confucian values in the United States. *Journal of Managerial Issues*, *12*(1), 34.

Rokeach, M. (1973). *The nature of human values*. New York: Free Press.

Schwartz, S. H. (Ed.), (1992). Vol. 25. *Universals in the content and structure of values: Theory and empirical tests in 20 countries*. New York: Academic Press.

Super, D. E. (1957). *The psychology of careers*. Vol. 195. New York: Harper & Row.

Thurstone, L. L. (1927). A law of comparative judgment. *Psychological Review*, *34*(4), 273–286.

Tsang, N. K. F. (2011). Dimensions of Chinese culture values in relation to service provision in hospitality and tourism industry. *International Journal of Hospitality Management*, *30*(3), 670–679. http://dx.doi.org/10.1016/j.ijhm.2010.12.002.

Tung, R. (2014). Research on Asia: Promise and perils. *Journal of Asia Business Studies*, *8*(3), 189–192. http://dx.doi.org/10.1108/JABS-03-2014-0025.

Warner, M., & Rowley, C. (2010). Chinese management at the crossroads: Setting the scene. *Asia Pacific Business Review*, *16*(3), 273–284.

Weng, Q., McElroy, J. C., Morrow, P. C., & Liu, R. (2010). The relationship between career growth and organizational commitment. *Journal of Vocational Behavior, 77*(3), 391–400.

Winzar, H. (2015). The ecological fallacy: How to spot one and tips on how to use one to your advantage. *Australasian Marketing Journal; AMJ, 23*(1), 86–92. http://dx.doi.org/10.1016/j.ausmj.2014.12.002.

World Values Survey. (2016). *World Values Survey wave 6 (2010–2014) OFFICIAL AGGREGATE*. Retrieved from: http://www.worldvaluessurvey.org/.

Yen, R. J. (2000). Racial stereotyping of Asians and Asian Americans and its effect on criminal justice: A reflection on the Wayne Lo case. *Asian American Law Journal, 7*, 1.

Zhu, Y., & Warner, M. (2000). An emerging model of employment relations in China: A divergent path from the Japanese? *International Business Review, 9*(3), 345–361.

CHAPTER 4

Corporate Authoritarianism and Civil Society Responding in Korea: The Case of Minority Shareholders' Movement*

G.-S. Park
Korea University, Seoul, South Korea

4.1 FALL OF THE MYTH OF CORPORATE AUTHORITARIANISM

The myth is no more, as the immortals have fallen. The myth of Korea's large business conglomerates being too large to ever fail is no more. As these mega-sized businesses started crumbling in the aftermath of the 1997 financial crisis, exposed were inner workings of these companies that had previously been hidden from the outside world. Fraudulent accounting practices were uncovered amongst many other irrational practices. No other example illustrates this event more than the 1999 fall of the Daewoo conglomerate. While Daewoo was not the first conglomerate to fall, the story of its epic demise is significant for several reasons. Daewoo was ranked among the very top of Korea's conglomerates, with its rise often positively touted as being most symbolic of the Korean developmental model of compressed growth. Yet, the size of its fraudulent accounting reached a total of 41 trillion Korean Won. In other words, Daewoo had lost roughly 2 trillion annually for the past 20 years, destroying any ounce of added value they seemingly created in the process.

Another myth that was destroyed at the time, to the dismay of many Koreans, was that the nation's banks would never fail. Prior to these events, few Koreans have ever considered the possibility that banks, which were the

---

*A different version of this chapter appeared in Park, Gil-Sung and Ha-Sung Jang. 2005. "Corporate Governance and Market Authority" (in Korean) in Cho, Dae-yeop and Gil-Sung Park eds., *Hankuksahoe ŏdirogana? (Where is Korean Society Headed to?)*. Seoul: Good Information.

symbol of financing during the days of developmental economics, would ever fail. Nevertheless, all five of the largest mega-sized banks in Korea fell without exception.[1] The bankruptcy of Korea's banks then became the turning point by which the effectiveness and rationale of the developmental economics era's conglomerate-centric finance market and government-led financing came under scrutiny.

The reputation garnered by big business during the age of authoritarian rule was that of both strength and simplicity. The image and authority of the company owner often was equated with those of the company itself. Hence, the fate of the company was a direct function of the company owner's method of management. As such, the myths associated with a company's rise in Korea were pretty much those of its owners, as opposed to the stories of professional managers elsewhere around the world. These myths in Korea spoke neither of organizational structures nor branding successes, but merely the paternalistic presence of, for example, Kim Woo-choong at Daewoo and Chung Ju-young at Hyundai. The formation of this paternalistic ownership structure that has also been a mainstay of the Korean economy for so long dates back to the 1970s. This structure of corporate governance continued without much change until the 1997 financial crisis.

The market power in Korean society, which should have been accompanied by societal acceptance based upon guidelines of fairness, was greatly damaged by crony capitalism. Companies were relying on rigid business networks and building corporate governance structures that were lacking transparency and responsibility. Investment risks that should have stayed in the realm of the company were being shifted towards society by a system of luring the public to take on risks, even as the profits made from such investments were often not shared with those outside the company. This system of using society to hedge risks unfortunately encouraged companies to often take part in business ventures that may yield profit but not so much productivity gains (Kim & Im, 2000, p. 8). Within the framework of crony capitalism that was rampant, companies expanded its reach by often poaching the government or plundering banks, making it difficult

---

[1] The five major banks prior to the financial crisis were Cheil Bank, Hanil Bank, Choheung Bank, Sangup Bank, and Wehwan Bank. Both Hanil and Sangup are currently out of business, while Cheil was sold to foreign investors, Choheung was sold to Shinhan Financial Group, and Wehwan was sold to a foreign bank, resulting in not one of the big five surviving in its original state.

for rational market power to properly function. Meanwhile, civil society had no structure to counter such problems. As a result, society's trust in the business sector narrowed, and social norms and value systems were beginning to be adversely affected by this mistrust. In retrospect, the structural flaws in business practices were accelerating the clock towards a fall of the conglomerates, even as nobody predicted the downfall of the so-called immortals. The structural flaws, of course, were revealed all too strongly when Korea was dragged through the worldwide transformations of globalization, information revolution, democratization, as well as the 1997 financial crisis.

The 1997 financial crisis forced Korea to implement a severance with past history, as the country before and after the crisis showed completely different patterns. The crisis compelled Korea to throw away the developmental models from the previous era and forcefully adopt a new era of restructuring, based upon new frameworks for reform and conflict resolution. The financial crisis also made Koreans disapprove its own past. The International Monetary Fund's (IMF) manual for restructuring forced Korean society to cut its ties with the past and make changes to, but not limited to, its economic structure. The IMF asked the country to throw away its past practices not only relating to government, business, finance, and labor, but also daily customs in the Koreans' way of life. Korean value systems and attitudes were also asked to be changed. The resulting disassembling of society proceeded at an enormous pace. In the process, the Korean self-identity was shaken to its roots, even taking a devastating toll on social trust that used to be a collateral for mature social relationships in the past. In particular, the public's trust toward large conglomerates and government sunk to a level that made one doubt whether there was any mechanism at all that would prevent total anarchy in the near future. This trend eventually led to a rationale among Koreans that any entity that cannot guarantee livelihood of the individual should be abandoned, whether that entity is the nation, tradition, political party, or the government, resulting in a wide spread phenomena of postnationalism, posttradition, postgovernment, postorganization, and postauthority in Korea (Park, 2003).

Amidst these processes, the authoritarianism of past was dismantled quickly, yet without a new paradigm of authority to take its place. Authoritarianism in Korean society stems from both its socio-cultural roots in Confucianism, which is a symbol of a canon-based culture that justified authoritarian human relationship as well as the system of

state-led modernization in which the resources were mobilized under a strict hierarchical chain that was implemented with coercion (Park, 2008, pp. 129–130).

Although the oppressive and unilateral authoritarian politics was thought to have somehow gone via the process of democratization, the country lacked the reasonable institutions and new authority to deal with the social conflicts that were to come. The Korean society now experienced several eruptions within business, organizations, intelligentsia, educational institutions, and the family that is most likely due to this lack of new authority. Conventional authoritarianism had no place in Korean society any more, and nowhere did this statement ring truer than in the political arena. The problem here is that even as the authoritarianism of the past was undergoing dissolution, Korea had a hard time finding a new structure of authority to replace the old one. Nevertheless, the one thing that stood true was that the new authority would never be able to form without the consent of or shared governance of civil society.

Large companies were never free from such sea changes in Korean society. In fact, some would argue that in several ways the large companies were at the core of the dissolution of old authoritarianism. This argument is strengthened when considering the endless stream of debates in society about corporate governance as a tool to protect the stakeholders of large companies. As discussion on corporate governance evolved over time, the values of transparency and responsibility emerged as the main principles for evaluating corporate governance. Simultaneously, corporate governance expanded its reach from originally concerning only the welfare of company stakeholders to all aspects of Korean society itself: leading to the rationale that a company's responsibility extends to the society within which it operates. Accordingly, companies were asked to expand its responsibility from the most basic and general function of creating added value for the company itself to adding value to the social community within which it is a member. Hence, the terms, corporate social responsibility and socially responsible investment rose to become keywords for the companies of our time.

4.2 THE UNFOLDING OF MINORITY SHAREHOLDERS' MOVEMENT

The minority shareholders' movement has become the most symbolic and representative case of civil society activism in the process of social restructuring following the 1997 financial crisis (Park & Kim, 2008, p. 59). The financial

crisis has meant not only a comprehensive restructuring process at the institutional level but also a halt to the Korean way of thought and practice (Park & Kim, 2005, p. 37). The historical context of the country having just experienced a financial crisis also laid fertile ground for the growth of activist groups and their activities, as Korean society's corruption, incompetence, absurdity, irrationality, and inefficiency were all exposed. Hence, the activist groups were able to investigate the causes for the crisis as well as present alternatives for resolution, by explicating those responsible (Hong, 2000, p. 124). They had emerged as the morally superior and trustworthy alternative, in relative terms, to the untrustworthy governmental, political, and market-based establishment of Korea. In this vein, the Non-governmental Organizations (NGOs) were able to gain legitimacy as the bastion of reform in Korea, while their work on minority shareholders' rights was perceived as true economic reform (Park & Kim, 2008, p. 60).

The minority shareholders' movement ultimately has its objective in the reform or reorganization of the shareholder-centric corporate governance structure, as opposed to the traditional owner-centric or executive-centric structures (Park & Kim, 2008, p. 62). The movement was organized to protect the interests of minority shareholders by way of consolidating the otherwise scattered separate votes (Jang, 1997, p. 2). In other words, tyrannical administrative practices of business executives were to be checked and accountability called for in the case of bad management, in order to protect the interests of minority shareholders. Hence, such a movement is perhaps the most democratic and capitalistic means of public interest advancement within the market economy. The minority shareholders' movement in its essence is a means toward individual interests of each shareholder yet results in promoting the openness and transparency of a corporation as well. This, in turn, enhances the role of the capital market in market mechanisms. In essence, this logic is a very useful and convenient way for minority shareholders to assert their rights that are too often eclipsed by the tyranny of large shareholders. All the while, it promotes public interest alongside the private interest of shareholders (Kim, 1999, pp. 60–61).

On Jul. 24, 1998, an occurrence unthinkable to the conventional mind took place in that minority shareholders had just won a lawsuit against the executives of Cheil Bank. The 52 minority shareholders, organized by the People's Solidarity for Participatory Democracy (PSPD), brought the current and past executives of Cheil Bank to court by way of Korea's first ever derivative suit. The final verdict was the court asking

the executives to reimburse shareholders an amount of 40 billion Korean Won. The next day, this court decision became the top news of all the major daily newspapers. The significance of this ruling lies in its foreshadowing of the great transformation that was to take place in Korea's corporate governance. The ruling effectively set a first ever precedent for minority shareholders holding corporate executives responsible for illegal business practices. The background to this ruling goes back to Jan. 1997, which was well before the financial crisis. The aforementioned PSPD had decided to address Cheil Bank's illegal loans and criminal actions by its executives in regard to the Hanbo Steel Company, to which Cheil was the primary bank. PSPD gathered minority shareholders and attended Cheil's February shareholders' meeting in order to officially raise the issue of the executives' responsibility. These series of events led to the Jun. 1997 legal actions.

PSPD followed up its legal victory against Cheil Bank with action in Jun. 1997 against Samsung Electronics by requesting annulment of the company's convertible bonds and to bring the executives to court for forgery of board of directors' meeting minutes. The assertion by PSPD was that the convertible bonds issued by Samsung Electronics were overwhelmingly favorable toward Lee Jae Yong, the son of the Samsung conglomerate Lee Kun Hee, which in the end caused much harm to both the company and its minority shareholders. In addition, there was no board of directors' agreement to issue the convertible bonds in question, thus the supposed decision that there was an agreement among directors was forged, according to PSPD. In Oct. 1998, PSPD also brought forth a derivative suit against Chairman Lee Kun Hee and 10 other top Samsung executives for providing illegal political campaign funds as well as another related to appropriate funding of affiliated companies.[2]

Nevertheless, PSPD's march towards changing corporate governance in Korea was not all smooth. In Jun. of 1997, a mega-sized problem erupted as Kia Motors went bankrupt. Koreans knew Kia, at the time, as the people's company that had no large shareholders, unlike the other conglomerates. Once Kia went bankrupt, civil society groups mobilized a movement to purchase Kia Motors shares in order to save the company, yet PSPD refused to take part on the grounds that Kia already had its shareholders and that

---

[2] The legal suit brought against Samsung Electronics resulted in a win for the minority shareholders, as the court told Samsung to reimburse 97.7 billion Korean Won to them.

there can be no such thing as a "people's company." Although PSPD was generally on the side of the weak actors in society, they judged that the labor unions and business executives were not weak actors in this particular case. This decision brought upon much criticism from both within and outside PSPD. As a result, they were simultaneously involved in the fighting with Samsung, a standoff with other civil society groups regarding Kia Motors, and managing a soured relationship with labor unions.

In Dec. 1997, the financial crisis erupted and the problem of Korea's large conglomerates' underdeveloped governance structure became a matter of public debate, exonerating some of PSPD's past actions and its implication towards the Korean economy. Soon, private investors in Korea as well as foreign institutional investors started voluntarily delegating their funds to PSPD. That profit-seeking investors would delegate their shares to a civil society organization meant that the securing of transparency and responsibility in business practices was not only a matter of preserving economic value but also creating social value. However, the domestic institutional investors decided to ignore PSPD's activities in favor of continuing to work with large conglomerate executives, effectively going in the opposite direction from domestic individual or foreign institutional investors. The main reason behind this is the domestic institutions' inability to escape the influence of the large business conglomerates in Korea.

PSPD accepted the delegation of shares upon three conditions. One is that the agenda is set by PSPD itself. No shares were accepted to further the interests of a particular shareholder, whether domestic or foreign. The same conditions were applied even to labor unions, as all requests that were not in favor of all, as opposed to some, shareholders were refused. Another condition for accepting delegation was independence of funding source. All finances were supported by individual donations with no support received from shareholders, government, nor the business sector. The other condition was that all agenda items are defined as those that serve the interest of the company and shareholders as a whole. Items that do not adhere to this principle are never touched. It is within this context that the financial crisis brought upon a change in perception. For the first time ever, people spoke of the need to protect the shareholder or the creditor. These discussions were not limited to the field of corporate governance but also became the core agenda item for reforming Korea's economic structure as a whole. Because this process had to do with the interests of pretty much everyone, nobody actively raised much fuss about this process, other than some civil society groups.

Soon enough, the government announced the need to improve corporate governance based upon the request of the IMF. Accordingly, principles concerning the reform of large conglomerates in Korea were prepared. The so-called 5+3 principle was announced where five basic principles for companies' structural adjustment was announced in Jan. 1998 to reform the four areas of finance, industry, labor, and public sector. The five included: improvement of transparency, ban on mutual debt guarantees, reform of financial structures, strengthening of core competencies, and strengthening of the responsibility of controlling shareholders and management. In Aug. 1999, the government and business sectors agreed to the "Three supplemental measures as follow-up to business conglomerate reform." This consisted of a ban on business conglomerates from dominating non-banking sectors, revival of the regulation for limiting the total amount of investment, the blocking of illegal internal transactions, and curbing irregular inheritance. In the end, the 5+3 principles of corporate governance were pretty much the collection of corporate governance-related demands that were requested by civil society groups.

Conventional wisdom dictates that the strengthening of a market economy is brought upon by the reduction of government involvement. However, in the case of Korea, the government intervened in the aftermath of the crisis because they deemed the market forces were not operating effectively. In addition, because both the market and government had not been able to properly perform its functions, civil society decided to join forces with the market itself. That these civil society groups brought legal action against the nation's largest economic power in Samsung and Chairman Lee Kun Hee, influenced corporate reform policies, and received support from domestic and foreign investors was a shock to both the market and government alike. The impetus behind the real changes brought upon by PSPD was less the visible participation in shareholders' meetings but the legal actions it took to assert its legal rights. They chose the strategy of bringing about permanent institutional change by seeking court verdicts against Cheil Bank and Samsung Electronics. Such a strategy required much professionalism, time, and effort, which in itself was quite different from the civic action Korea had been used to at the time. In the end, legal victories were able to bring about much stronger change than any government-led efforts for reform.

As such, it is impossible not to mention the role civil society played in changing corporate governance. In addition, the financial crisis served as an opportunity for government to reset its relationship with civil society.

In its most extreme expression, it would not be wrong to state that civil society groups played the central role in bringing about changes in Korea's corporate governance structure.

4.3 CHANGES IN CORPORATE GOVERNANCE STRUCTURE

Most eminent changes in corporate governance is the fact that new rules were made: introduction of the system of outside directors, introduction of the recommendation committee for outside directors, introduction of auditing committee, strengthening of minority shareholders' rights, strengthening the system of public announcements, ban on mutual shareholding, system of limiting the total amount of investment, abolishing limitations on foreign investors, allowing of hostile mergers & acquisitions, introduction of the establishment of holding companies, and the establishment of the Securities Supervisory Board.

The rights of minority shareholders was also strengthened, as the rights to representative suits and injunction, convocation of extraordinary shareholders' meetings, shareholders' right to proposals, concentrated vote systems, dismissal of board members or auditors, access to accounting records, and appointment of auditors were all strengthened. As represented in Table 4.1, the conditions for exercising all these rights were relaxed significantly between 1997 and 2015. In other words, the barriers for minority shareholders to exercise rights are now significantly lowered. For example, in regards to the right to representative suits, the minimum number of shares to exercise the right was lowered from 1% share ownership in 1997 to 0.005% in 2015.[3]

The internal organization of companies also changed according to the new corporate governance structure. Most important among these changes is the board of directors, an entity that in past had little power, suddenly rose to prominence as the true managers of a company. In the past, there had been little separation between company managers and the board of directors. Whereas in the past, executives would have titles such as managing director or executive director that encompassed both the executive and board of directors, now only members of the board of directors are allowed to use the term director. The introduction of outside directors also

---

[3]Representative suits are public interest suits where an individual shareholder takes legal action on behalf of the interest of all shareholders, thus many advanced nations such as the United States or Japan have no limitation on the right to suits, as long as at least one share is owned by that person, based upon the principle of equality among shareholders.

Table 4.1 Shares need to exercise minority shareholders' rights

	1997	2002	2007	2012	2015
Right to representative suits by shareholders	1% (0.5%)	0.01%	0.005%	0.005%	0.005%
Rights to injunction	1% (0.5%)	0.05% (0.025%)	0.025% [0.0125%]	0.025% [0.0125%]	0.025% [0.0125%]
Right to request convocation of extraordinary general meeting of shareholders	3% (1.5%)	3% (1.5%)	1.5% [0.75%]	1.5% [0.75%]	1.5% [0.75%]
Shareholder's right to make proposals	1% (0.5%)	1% (0.5%)	0.5% [0.25%]	0.5% [0.25%]	0.5% [0.25%]
Right to request cumulative voting	–	3%	3%	3%	3%
Right to demand removal of director or auditor	1% (0.5%)	0.5% (0.25%)	0.25% [0.125%]	0.25% [0.125%]	0.25% [0.125%]
Shareholder's right to inspect books of account	3% (1.5%)	0.1% (0.05%)	0.05% [0.025%]	0.05% [0.025%]	0.05% [0.025%]
Right to request court-appointed inspector	3% (1.5%)	3% (1.5%)	1.5% [0.75%]	1.5% [0.75%]	1.5% [0.75%]

Notes: Stakes inside parentheses "()" apply to companies capitalized at over 100 billion Korean Won. Stakes inside brackets "[]" apply to financial investors as ordained by presidential decree.
Commercial Act, Security & Exchange Act, and Capital Market Act [enacted 2007].

brought about many real changes. In spite of the fact that many of the outside directors brought into the board had preexisting amicable relations with company officials, thereby threatening the independence of the board, the fact that outside directors were made to share the same legal responsibilities as internal directors acted as a failsafe mechanism in the event that an outside director acted in the unilateral and improper interest of a company official. The semi-official office of structural reform replaced the company chairman's secretariat, which in the past acted as an arbitrary corporate governance organization. In addition, the past practice of company heads not registering as part of the board of directors for the purpose of avoiding legal responsibility was fixed to have the head register as an official board member during the Kim Dae-Jung administration.

Corporate governance structure in Korea eventually showed signs of change, especially with the large business conglomerates. It is interesting to note that the conglomerates' new corporate governance reforms proceeded in many different forms, which can be summed up into five different types: (1) keeping the traditional business leadership intact, (2) transforming into a holding company, (3) transforming into a small group-led system, (4) privatized former public enterprises, and (5) all affiliates going independent. The forms of corporate governance-induced change exhibited by the large business conglomerates show quite the variety.

Nevertheless, the problems of corporate governance still persist, as can be found in various government data. With shares owned by the company head's family reducing from 9.54% in 1997 to 5.09% in 2015, it may seem that things have gotten better, yet closer examination reveals that is not necessarily true. The smaller number of the owner family shares have been offset by the increase in mutual ownership between affiliated companies via cross-shareholding, resulting in an even stronger leverage in the hands of the heads. The actual controlling share of the company head in 2015 is 52.95%, which is a significant increase from the 39.57% in 1997. In other words, although the company head's personally owned shares have dropped over the years, the actual leverage the head has over company decisions have increased when taking into account internal shares owned by special affiliates, treasury stock, and owners association shares.

4.4 CORPORATE GOVERNANCE AS A GLOBAL AGENDA: NOT LIMITED TO KOREA

The issue of corporate governance in Korea in the aftermath of the financial crisis had always been associated with social discourse on reform. This is

natural when considering that the large conglomerates were touted as one of the culprits of the crisis, as it is also natural to have strong pressure from society towards reforming their corporate governance. In response, the conglomerates did show a variety of responses, at least on the outside, to the very strong demands placed upon them by civil society and government. Whatever the truths or falsehoods are behind Korean companies' attempts at reform, there can be no denying that it brought upon many changes to its corporate governance. Whether it was caused by internal family dynamics, privatization of public enterprises, or social pressure for transparency of business practices, change did take place. Yet, it would be a big mistake to think such change was unique to Korea. The relevance of corporate governance was definitely not limited to this country, which had to undergo an IMF-led governance regime after a major financial crisis. In other words, improving corporate governance had been a common issue among many countries operating within the system of global capitalism.

Table 4.2 shows changes in corporate governance among Asian countries in 1997 and 2003, the so-called period of Asian financial crisis. When examining the practice of outside board directors, only Hong Kong, Malaysia, and Singapore among Asian countries had such a system in 1997 when the financial crisis hit. In regards to audit committees, only Malaysia and Singapore had such a system. Yet in 2003, most countries have adopted these two systems that are most representative of good corporate governance. All of East Asia had gone through corporate reforms. Of course, implementing

Table 4.2 Changes in corporate governance among Asian countries

Country	1997 Outside board members	1997 Audit committee	2003 Outside board members	2003 Audit committee
China			Y	Y
Hong Kong	Y		Y	Y
India			Y	Y
Indonesia			Y	Y
Malaysia	Y	Y	Y	Y
Philippines			Y	Y
Singapore	Y	Y	Y	Y
Korea			Y	Y
Taiwan			Y	Y
Thailand			Y	Y

Barton, Coombes, & Wong, 2004.

new systems of governance is an institutional prerequisite for countries whose economy depends upon capital infusion from other countries. It could be viewed as a mimetic process for the purpose of claiming legitimacy. Korea, which submitted itself to the IMF's governance regime following the crisis, experienced a coercive isomorphism, particularly as requested by international financial institutions, credit rating agencies, and foreign capital. However, countries that did not go directly under the knife of international financial institutions' governance regimes had the option of a mimetic isomorphism, as a method of instituting corporate governance, because it was judged to be the best standard response toward its own uncertain future. In summary, although the motivation and background to adopting corporate governance may have been different, in the end all countries did end up choosing to implement the isomorphic form of it.

Nevertheless, there is yet huge differences in corporate governance structure among Asian countries. A comparative figure of corporate governance across countries is represented in Table 4.3. According to the internationally respected figures published by the Institute of Management Development (IMD) and World Economic Forum (WEF), Korea's corporate governance ranks near the bottom. Although there are problems with the research method itself, the end result is a very negative opinion from the international society about Korean companies' corporate governance.

4.5 CONCLUSION: THE AUTHORITY OF BUSINESS TOWARDS NEW GOVERNANCE

This chapter addressed the rise of NGOs becoming pivotal actors in society after the 1997 financial crisis. In particular, the minority shareholders' movement and its resulting social implications were examined as their most representative activity on their way to becoming the standard for change. By asserting strong uncompromising voices against big capital, the minority shareholders' movement was able to provide Korean civil society with many possibilities for reform.

It is widely recognized that the minority shareholders' movement gave birth to many new possibilities and potentials toward civil society in Korea. With political parties in Korea yet inadequate to represent the grassroots interests of the masses, the activist groups served the function of quasi-political parties in their place. Over the years, the alliance between the state and market forces that developed throughout the period of the developmental state had revealed problems, notably ending up serving only the interests

Table 4.3 Asian countries ranked on corporate governance, 2003

Country	WEF Corporate governance	IMD			
		Independent board	Value on shareholders	Inside trading	Shareholders rights
Singapore	8	4	3	4	7
Hong Kong	13	6	10	16	10
Malaysia	21	9	7	21	27
Taiwan	23	17	35	35	30
Japan	31	53	59	14	58
India	32	37	48	55	38
Korea	33	58	54	45	57
Philippines	43	42	45	53	53
China	44	32	46	52	54
Indonesia	46	55	57	56	56

Notes: The WEF survey was conducted 49 countries in 2003. The IMD survey was conducted 59 countries in 2003.
WEF, IMD Competitiveness Report 2003.

and extended rule of those with power or capital. The lack of public sector mechanisms to monitor, criticize, and check eventually threatened the system of capitalism in Korea itself. The NGOs and their activities such as the minority shareholders' movement, based upon the motto of economic democratization, provided the initial step for resolving the issues pending in Korean society (Park & Kim, 2008: 60–1).

Corporate governance structure is emerging as an important topic that may decide the business ethics in Korean society. Since the 1997 financial crisis, the topic of corporate governance had always been the front and center of public debates. Over time, there have been many changes to corporate governance structure in Korea. Civil society groups have certainly played their part, much aided by the sea changes taking place on a global level as well as aided by the urgency created by the economic crisis that took place in Korea. Within this dynamism, new rules on governance structures were made, while minority shareholders rights were strengthened and internal structures at large Korean companies were also changed much in order to improve corporate governance. It is also worthwhile to note the diverse forms of corporate governance structure emerging from and evolving within different companies.

However, the owner-centric hierarchy, which had traditionally been at the heart of the businesses and needing to improve corporate governance, actually showed signs of strengthening, still contributing much to Koreans negative sentiment towards big businesses. Nevertheless, it would be wrong to pigeonhole Koreans as being anticorporate, as evidence on Koreans' enormous respect for professional businessmen and positive evaluation of large conglomerates' role in the economy suggests the opposite. Negative survey results can be explained less by anticorporate sentiment but more as dissatisfaction with the backward corporate governance structure.

The reason corporate governance is so important in predicting the road ahead for Korean society is because its value is not limited to mere maximization of company worth: corporate governance is an important variable whose function leads to no less than the creation of values in society itself. This is due to the preconditions of corporate governance in transparency and responsibility having direct ties with social values. This is proven by noting the amazing almost identical findings between corruption indexes and corporate governance indexes, in spite of the fact that the two use different units of measurement. Such is no coincidence.

In the aftermath of the financial crisis, the restructuring of society by the state, market, and civil society created dynamism that was very different

from the previous. The result was one where civil society would shed its former role of all out standoffs with the government in favor of maintaining a constant and balanced tension with the government. The government and business that used to speak in the same voice during the age of developmental economics were now speaking in different terms. That civil society and the state were able to transition from conflict and confrontation to speaking in unison is clear evidence that new governance is forming. Now, there is a flexible system within which both disagreement and cooperation between civil society and state coexists.

For the future, Korea's task at hand is to form a structure where the state, market, and civil society can have a healthy tension with one another based on introspection. The practice of excessive interference by state into the market that was born from compressed growth, excessive market-centric measures that concentrate too much on efficiency of the market economy, and civil society groups that declared its legitimacy based upon none but challenges to authority are all problems that require introspection and resolution. Korea needs a new governance structure that preserves a healthy balance between government, business, and civil society groups. It will be unlikely that any market authority or business authority will be possible without the consent of civil society.

The age of globalization bestows upon businesses both social responsibility and social leadership. In accordance, the boundaries of what constitutes interested parties to a business seem expanding without limit. Businesses can decide to transcend their most immediate and general responsibility of creating added economic value to actively embrace the wider responsibility of preserving sustainable social communities. Only then, will the new market authority and business ethics truly blossom.

REFERENCES

Barton, D., Coombes, P., & Wong, S.C.-Y. (2004). Asia's governance challenge. *The McKinsey Quarterly, 2*, 54–61.

Fair Trade Commission Republic of Korea. (2015). *2015 Annual report*. Seoul: Korea Fair Trade Commission.

Hong, I.-P. (2000). Ije dasi witaeroun mohŏmŭi kiroe sŏn hankuk siminundong (Korean civic movement on the edge of dangerous adventure). *Kyŏngjewa*, (45), 114–131.

Jang, H.-S. (1997). Soaekjuju kwolniundongŭi ŭiŭiwa silchŏnbangan (The meaning of minority shareholder activism and a plan of practice). In People's Solidarity for Participatory Democracy (Ed.), *Soaekjuju kwonliundonge kwanhan jŏngchaektoronhoe jaryojip (Minority shareholder activism policy forum proceedings)*. Seoul: PSPD.

Kim, E.-Y. (1999). Soaekjoojoowoondongŭi heŭlŭumkwa jŏnmang (The current and prospects of minority shareholder activism). *Sidaeinsik*, (30), 52–61.

Kim, B.-K., & Im, H.-B. (2000). Dongasia jungshiljabonjui ui shinhwawa hyunshil: Hanguk, Daeman, Taeguk (Myth and reality of crony capitalism in East Asia: Korea, Taiwan and Thailand). *Kyegan Sasang, 45*, 7–74.

Park, G.-S. (2003). *Hanguk sahoe ui chae kujohwa: kangyodoen chojong, kaltungjok choyul (Restructuring of Korean society: Forced adjustments and contentious coordinations)*. Seoul: Korea University Press.

Park, G.-S. (2008). Korean society caught in post-authoritarian trap. In K.-D. Kim (Ed.), *Social change in Korea* Seoul: Jimoondang.

Park, G.-S., & Kim, E. A. (2005). Changes in attitude toward work and workers' identity in Korea. *Korea Journal, 45*(3), 36–57.

Park, G.-S., & Kim, K.-P. (2008). Financial crisis and minority shareholders' movement in Korea: The unfolding and social consequences of the movement. *Korean Journal of Sociology, 42*(8), 59–76.

CHAPTER 5

Business Ethics in Korea: Chaebol Dynastic Practices and the Uneven Transition From a Market to an Entrepreneurial Mode of Exchange

B. Dalton, M. dela Rama
University of Technology Sydney, Ultimo, NSW, Australia

5.1 INTRODUCTION

Challenging the neoclassical view that the market is somehow distinct from society, sociologist John Lie (1992a) developed a concept of "modes of exchange" that views markets as embedded in social relations. Lie developed four typologies of modes of exchange (i.e., market, manorial, mercantile, and entrepreneurial) that differ according to the degrees to which trade is open or closed (socially) and whether the market is intraregional or interregional. We argue that in the period of rapid economic and social transformation between 1953 and the late 1990s, there was no linear or clearly staged trajectory from one mode of exchange to another. Instead, manorial, mercantile and, more recently, market and entrepreneurial modes coexisted in Korea. In this paper, we briefly discuss the relevance of these typologies to South Korea's postwar economic development and focus specifically on how modes of market exchange have interacted with the ways political and economic elites have socially constructed the concept of business ethics.

Specifically, decades of coexisting mixed modes of exchange have created uncertainly with regards to the "rules of the game," including how they applied to the behavior of political and economic elites. Korea's elites could more easily rationalize and justify certain practices by seeking support from each other to not only justify "growth at all costs," but also to refashion elements within Korea's rich cultural traditions in ways that served their own purposes. But as the economy and democracy have matured, Korea has become more deeply embedded in the global economy and, inevitably,

more exposed to exogenous economic shocks. In the context of this transition from a mercantile to a market or entrepreneurial mode of exchange, some rules of the game are shifting, and political and economic elites' past justification strategies are increasingly being challenged. This creates new dilemmas for the *chaebol* at a time when they are attempting to both professionalize their management practices while also holding on to structures of the past, in particular the maintenance of family ownership by passing on *chaebol* ownership from father to son.

5.2 KOREAN DEVELOPMENT DURING MIXED MODES OF EXCHANGE

Lie (1992a) criticized the orthodox view of the market as being asocial and unqualified and presented a sociological account of the market in which economic development can experience different modes of exchange. In the application of his concept, he accounted for conflicts and power structures within different modes of exchange and markets as being based on power, stratification, and class. The underlying social structure provides the parameter within which modes coexist, dominate, or disappear. Thus in certain periods, particularly when there are struggles for popular or elite control, we can see the coexistence of competing modes of exchange (Lie, 1992b). Lie's emphasis on how power struggles among groups for control over trade, rather than individual utility maximization, is highly relevant to processes at play in Korea's postwar economic development.

In Korea, the period between 1953 and the late 1990s saw rapid economic and social transformation. During this time, there was no linear or clearly staged trajectory from one mode of exchange to another. Instead features of manorial, mercantile and, more recently, entrepreneurial modes coexisted. For example, elements of the manorial mode (e.g., markets operated under the control of local elites, economic activities were aligned with dominant interests, and local economic activities were oriented to an interregional division of labor) were all features of the Korean economy, particularly in the immediate decades following the Korean War (1950–53).

This period also saw the rise of the mercantile mode of exchange. During an extended period of authoritarian rule and extensive state intervention in the economy, mercantile elites emerged and became closely connected to the central political authority as a way of maintaining their privileged position. During this period, the Korean government channeled massive amounts of capital through subsidies and low-interest-rate loans

into trusted *chaebols*. These favored firms also enjoyed trade preferences and monopoly rights, among other indulgences, extended by Korea's political elites (Oh & Varcin, 2002).

While such preferential treatment enabled the *chaebol* to grow into massive business empires, government support came at a price. State bureaucrats were willing to provide this largesse, including business permits or legal protection to market actors, only if businesses or business owners remitted payments to the former. In this context Oh and Varcin (2002) argue that the Korean state operated in many ways like a "Mafioso State" in that it ran a protection "racket," where Korea's "market actors are forced to give up the option of relying on prices or trust and rush to state bureaucrats for protection and access to State-owned banks' capital" (714).

More recently, however, elements of market and entrepreneurial modes have emerged. Korea has become a key component of a complex ecology of interrelated international markets where the development and fluctuations of one market have repercussions on other markets. The implications of this transition became most obvious in the aftermath of two major international financial crises, the Asian financial crisis in 1997–98 and the global financial crisis in 2008. The fallout from these crises exposed a weak and poorly-regulated financial system, wildly overleveraged firms, and occasionally corrupt corporate governance practices. In particular, it highlighted how the intricate web of cross-share holding arrangements within *chaebols* had served as an expedient tool for owner-manager to facilitate the inheritance and donation of their property, support insolvent affiliates, and circumvent regulations (Jung, 2004). While the governments under Kim Daejung (1998–2002), Lee Myeongbak (2008–13), and Pak Geunhye (2013–) responded by undertaking significant reforms (e.g., closing highly indebted banks, forced resolution of bankrupt companies, strengthening of previously inept financial regulation, and the banning of cross-shareholdings among affiliates), serious weaknesses remain.

Korea's experience of mixed modes of exchange has created uncertainty with regard to the "rules of the game," particularly as they relate to what constitutes ethical or unethical political or corporate behavior. In this context, Korean elites sought to rationalize and justify certain practices by turning to each other for support and, in particular, for endorsement of the argument that the ends—economic growth—justifies the means, namely, authoritarian rule, extensive market intervention, and questionable business practices. This paper further shows that both sets of elites have supported the other by arguing that such practices are acceptable because they have their roots in Korea's cultural, in particular Confucian, tradition.

5.3 "OUR ACTIONS ARE JUSTIFIABLE BECAUSE THEY DELIVER ECONOMIC GROWTH"

Business ethics represents a fluid concept, as what makes a behavior "ethical" may not be fixed or intrinsic, but may rather be an interpretation imposed on behavior. As such, "business ethics" can be seen as a social construct, the result of an individual or collective interpretation of a certain social phenomenon through discourse in a specific setting (Berger & Luckmann, 1966). In a period of political and economic transition, the concept of business ethics becomes even more fluid. Often accompanying rapid change is uncertainty as well as a variety of definitions for ethics and related concepts of corruption, justice, and fairness (or alternative moralities). With such diverse interpretations of business ethics, we may find it easier to disguise or rationalize conduct as, depending on the point of view, an action can be found to be morally acceptable and ethically corrupt at the same time.

In this way, the coexistence of different modes of market exchange can create uncertainty and undermine the building of a normative consensus regarding what constitutes an ethical way to do business. In established modes of exchange, conceptions of ethics (and related distinctions between private and public) may be sufficiently settled for more clear-cut behavior classifications to apply. But in transitional societies, matters are more unsettled. Debates over what constitutes an ethical or unethical action are more explicitly linked to other debates over what is the most "legitimate" economic and political model. Here, meanings of associated values of a preferred economic and political model have yet to be fully incorporated into the legal system and institutionalized in the political process. Findings by Hao and Johnston (1995) in their study of corruption in China in the 1990s are relevant in this regard, specifically, that the level of contestation around the meaning of corruption tended to be particularly acute in mainland Chinese society in the 1990s because it was experiencing major economic and political change (pp. 80–94). According to the study, debates may be over:

> …the boundaries between public and private roles, institutions, and resources; the boundaries between state and society; and the distinction between individual and collective interest and rights; the distinction between politics and administration; and conflicts over the proper extent and limits of market, bureaucratic and patrimonial processes of allocation. (Hao & Johnston, 1995, p. 333)

For Korea's economic elites, the activities of influence-buying by private interests became normal, in the sense that it is not wrong because everyone

does it, and functional, in that it is instrumental to achieving an acceptable purpose (i.e., expansion and profit). For political elites, influence-peddling by politicians and bureaucrats were often viewed as necessary to discipline the *chaebol* to boost exports and thus realize a higher moral imperative, namely, that of rapid and significant economic growth.

Take for example, the reactions of many members of Korea's economic and political elite after two former presidents, Jeon Duhwan (1980–88) and No Tae-u (1987–92) were charged with corruption in August 1996. Corruption charges were based on allegations that President Jeon and No had illicitly accumulated and channeled more than US$1 billion and US$650 million, respectively, into personal slush funds while in office. Separately, several business tycoons had already been indicted on charges of paying bribes (disguised as political contributions) to the former presidents.

The two expresidents initially said that what they had done had served the national interest and, later in their trials, that the receipt of large contributions from business was a common political practice and, therefore, not wrong. Jeon regularly defended his "cooperation" with big business, including his receipt of large contributions, as being in the public interest as it contributed to the country's rapid economic development. In front of members of the National Assembly and a nationwide television audience, Jeon said that he had taken no money improperly from corporations during office, and while errors of judgment were made during his administration, he had little to apologize for. In his speech, he stated: "I worked closely with business to achieve rapid economic growth for our country" (cited in Clifford, 1997, p. 295).

After an investigation into No's financial affairs began in 1995, he emphasized that the collection of contributions from businessmen was a common feature of Korea's competitive political process in which all politicians were encouraged to solicit support and bestow favors to win elections. Shortly before his arrest, No argued that in this political context, his actions were excusable because the slush money was spent "for political purposes" and that such a large fund was necessary "considering the political and electoral culture" (*Korea Herald*, October 28, 1995). Early in his trial, No said: "everybody was doing it, it was part of political life at that time" (Clifford, 1997).

As the above statements suggest, Korean politicians have typically tried to excuse political corruption as functional ("it is not wrong because it is good for the economy"), as an institutional privilege ("it is not wrong because other members accept it"), or as an institutional fault ("it is not wrong

because other members do it"). Many also argued that their actions were, to an extent, excusable because corruption was part of Korean political life, and that in order to succeed in politics, one must sometimes be prepared to behave corruptly ("it is wrong, but not that bad because we had to do it").

Meanwhile, the chairmen of giant conglomerates implicated in the presidential slush fund scandals claimed that they had no choice but to donate to the ruling party as it was the way business was always done and that it made economic sense at the time. For example, Hyundai's founder and honorary chairman, Jeong Juyeong, considered himself a "nationalist capitalist" and argued that the need to compete successfully in an intensely competitive international economic arena justified any failure of Korean capitalists to "project a sense of morality" (Jeong, 1986, p. 360). In his autobiography, Jeong wrote:

> There are no businessmen whose behavior is based solely on morality like religious men. If a businessman acts like a religious man, how can he undertake his responsibilities in the overseas market where the competition is intense? How can he win out over the advanced countries? If all businessmen were to project a sense of morality in [everything] they said and did like moralists and religious men, not a single one would be victorious in international competition (p. 353).

Although keen to bring an end to "money politics," many businessmen did not want anticorruption sentiment to fuel an anticorruption crusade. Some business leaders have expressed concern that the investigation and prosecution of businessmen and officials on corruption charges could have a negative impact on both the economy and Korea's international reputation. During the investigations into the collapse of the *chaebol* Hanbo, one Hanbo company executive said:

> There should be an objective re-evaluation of the justification and the possible side effects in the move to investigate numerous businessmen to find the details of political donations. Also there should be a sincere study on how far into the past we should go to find out about the political funds whether in the ruling or opposition parties. Where can we draw the line? (Choson Ilbo, May 26, 1997).

In this way, political and economic elites exhibited an interdependent relationship which led them to mutually reinforce the legitimacy of each other's practices: the state defended its behavior as ethical as it disciplined the *chaebols* to deliver economic growth, while the *chaebols* argued that the Korean economy would not have been propelled to the extent that it had if *chaebols* were not granted extensive privileges by the government. While the *chaebol*-state relationship was characterized by troubled interaction, it remained relatively stable. This was not so much a manifestation of a common

commitment to Korea's economic development or an appreciation of the superiority of the state-led development model, but rather the response of a financially dependent capitalist class attempting to avoid state punitive measures and gain concessions. Nevertheless, it led to mutual support for each group's ethical rationale and allowed each to pursue their respective objectives.

One manifestation of the mutual support provided by political and economic elites in the construction of business ethics is how senior *chaebol* figures have fared in the Korean justice system. It has been standard practice for *chaebol* heads to be given lenient sentences, followed by presidential pardons, when they are found guilty of crimes. Since 1990, the heads of seven of the 10 biggest *chaebols* have been convicted for bribery, tax-evasion, or embezzlement. All received presidential pardons, and all returned to management positions. For example, Samsung Chairman Lee Geunhui was found guilty of bribing officials and fined US$100 million in 2008. He was given a prison sentence, but was pardoned, ostensibly because he was an International Olympic Committee member and was central to Seoul's successful 2018 Winter Olympics bid (Pontell & Geis, 2010).

According to economist Kim Woo-chan, "When the courts are deciding on the sentences, they actually look at whether they have contributed to the Korean economy. The president takes into consideration what sort of job they do and how many jobs they can create, for example." (quoted in Hazlehurst, 2013). According to economist and shareholder activist Jang Ha-Sung, "When the economy was growing so fast, everything was justified" (quoted in Kirk, 2014).

5.4 "OUR ACTIONS ARE NORMAL AS THEY ARE PART OF KOREAN CULTURE"

Korea's patriarchal traditions have provided a readily available cultural vocabulary for those in business (and those in the business of dominating others). Political and economic elites have sought to justify their own interpretations of ethics by selectively evoking cultural, in particular Confucian, traditions. This process has been described by Williams (1977) as creating "an intentionally selective version of a shaping past and a preshaped present, which is then powerfully operative in the process of social and cultural definition" (p. 115).

Scholars such as Eckert (1993), Janelli and Yim (1993), and Deuchler (1992) suggest that Confucian ideals are often evoked (usually in reconstructed form) and then promoted as authentic in order to serve the

purposes of Korean elites, a process described as the "mutual constitution of Confucianism and capitalism in South Korea" (Janelli & Janelli, 1997). For example, owners of Korea's *chaebol* have attempted to use the "company is a family" metaphor as a way of promoting productivity and maintaining labor peace (Choi, 1993; Janelli & Yim, 1993).

Traditional norms and relationships were useful in obfuscating the line between customs such as gift-giving and bribery, as well as group loyalty and nepotism. Traditional concepts of power and Confucianism's humanistic tradition could also be linked to a relatively flexible approach to the application of the law to check the behavior of senior businessmen and government officials. For example, economic and political elites might seek to blame the culture of gift-giving for their having to find "discretionary funds."[1] This may be a case of blaming tradition to disguise attempts by politicians to distribute patronage as a way to consolidate power and by business to retain market privileges.

However, it is important to note that despite such arguably cynical elite constructions of ethical behavior, Korean cultural tradition was not consistent with such practices. Indeed, Korean cultural tradition was also the source of widespread questioning of the ethical standing of the *chaebol*. Confucian values of antimaterialism and the ideal that the ruler's legitimacy rests on his ability to meet exacting moral and ethical standards are central tenets to Confucian thought. For example, followers of Confucianism may consider it moral and virtuous to "know" (graciously accept) one's place in a rigid hierarchy, but this tradition also stressed self-cultivation, principally through classical education practices which encourage social mobility.

It is also important to acknowledge the complexity and internal inconsistencies within certain Korean traditions. Robinson (1991) noted that "[Korean] Confucianism contains within its canon contradictory impulses that support centralization of political power around a merit-based bureaucracy while also affirming ascriptive class distinctions in society" (p. 206). Also, Confucian norms have recognized that if the ruler has behaved wrongly, he loses his heavenly mandate to rule and his subjects have the

---

[1] In 1992, in an attempt to prove that a 200 million won donation from the Hanbo Housing Corporation was above board, Democratic Liberal Party member of the National Assembly, Lee Taeseop, provided a detailed account of his expenses. Lee's total monthly budget of nearly 50 million won (US$625,000) covered "flowers" for his district's weddings and funerals (8 million won), organizing meetings with civic and professional organizations (3 million won), and handouts of money and gifts to his constituents especially around Chuseok and Lunar New Year (Shim, 1992a, 1992b).

right to overthrow him. At the same time, Confucianism has also stressed that the most important virtue of a subject is loyalty to the king and that a king's immorality should be corrected with moral persuasion and education, not through punishment. In line with this, Palais (1996) argued that "Confucians might justifiably withdraw their loyalty from such an immoral ruler, but they might also feel that it was their duty to stick with him to lead him from immorality to morality" (p. 1004).

There are also conflicts between different traditions that coexist within the one culture. For example, Confucianism and Korean folk traditions, sometimes referred to as the "second tradition" which includes folk traditions (e.g., animistic spirit worship, shamanism, fortune telling, geomancy), are responsible for a certain egalitarian ethic in Korean popular village culture that was in conflict with Confucian values of Joseon elite society (Brandt, 1971).

This also assumes that Confucian virtues, such as strong family ties, the greater importance of community over individuals, and social cohesiveness, have remained intact. It is possible that ethical standards in contemporary Korea may also, to some extent, be linked to a cultural decline or dilution. This can be in the form of the weakening or abandonment of some traditional values, or the gradual disappearance of village-based community networks which made these traditional values operable. Furthermore, capitalism itself could have had destructive effects on Confucian virtues. For example, Yun (2010) argued that in contemporary Korea, the demographic imbalance in labor markets (in 2005, approximately 30% of the Korean elderly aged 65 years or older participated in labor markets, while only 70% of Koreans in the 25-to-29-year age range were economically active) departs from the Confucian ideal, where adult children play the breadwinning role and take care of their dependent older family members, and that this is an example of how "crony capitalism and growth absolutism" have eroded Confucian culture (p. 256).

It is important to recognize this process of reformulation when analyzing interpretations of business ethics in Korea. With capitalist industrialization and the associated urbanization, mass production, mass education, and mass communication, increasing numbers of the population were directly exposed to elites using cultural justification. But these processes have also led to the growth of greater contestation of these justifications from groups within Korean civil society. This contestation has become more acute as the Korean economy has reeled in the aftermath of the Asian financial crisis and global financial crisis. Numerous corporate collapses and economic

recession have highlighted how the Korean economy and its manorial/mercantile foundations were insufficient to withstand exogenous shocks that have come with being more deeply embedded in the global economy.

5.5 CORPORATE GOVERNANCE AND BUSINESS ETHICS POST-FINANCIAL CRISES

The 1997 Asian financial crisis unleashed forces that placed significant pressure on both the economic and cultural justifications that supported the mixed manorial/mercantile modes of exchange. During this period, the Korean economy's exposure to the vagaries of global capital highlighted how the *chaebols* and the state were not only structurally ill-prepared for an economic system that had the market mode of exchange at its core, but were also found to be wanting from an ethical perspective.

The fallout from this crisis highlighted the failure of the Korean state and *chaebol* to cope up in a globalized market characterized by the mobility of capital across countries facilitated by technological advances in information, communications, and financial instruments (Chang, 2003). This post-1997 period saw the collapse of one *chaebol* after another and finally of the economy itself, ultimately leading to Korea's application to the International Monetary Fund (IMF) for an emergency loan.

The Asian financial crisis and the collapse of a string of large *chaebols* heightened awareness that poorly-run and weakly-managed business groups needed to institute robust controls that promoted transparent and accountable decision-making (Faure, 2002; Reed, 2002; Trivellato, 2002). At the time of the crisis, the concentration of economic power and management culture of dynastic dictatorship in the *chaebols* saw the "too big to fail" (Kim, Hoskisson, Tihanyi, & Hong, 2004) nature of this private sector form of organization contribute to Korea's economic downturn. Characteristics once touted as the basis of the *chaebols*' success were now being reevaluated as factors behind their failure and the broader weaknesses in the Korean economy.

The troubles of the Korean *chaebol* during the crisis instigated an inward-looking search for reform. Reform was actively promoted by international financial institutions such as the IMF, the OECD, and the Asian Development Bank. But while political discourse embraced the notion of corporate reform and some important measures were initiated, such as internal improvement of some Korean *chaebols* (Derichs & Heberer, 2002), both crises did not result in fundamental, structural reform of the family-based

ownership model. Thus while the governments under Kim Daejung (1998–2002), Lee Myeongbak (2008–13), and Pak Geunhye (2013–) responded by undertaking significant reforms, such as the closing of highly indebted banks, the forced resolution of bankrupt companies, and the strengthening of previously inept financial regulation, serious weaknesses have remained.

Over a decade later, Korea still ranks relatively poor on corporate governance indices. A 2007 joint report by the Korea Development Institute and the World Bank found that of the 12 biggest Asian economies, Korea ranked 7th in corporate governance, tied with Indonesia and well behind India (Suh & Chen, 2007). It was ranked 29th by Governance Metrics International (2010) among 39 countries in 2010, and according to research by the Asian Corporate Governance Association Korea (2012), Korea ranks well below other OECD countries in terms of standards corporate governance and shareholder rights.

These comparatively low international rankings have served to reinforce the notion of the "Korea discount," where foreign investors' and media's distrust and Korean companies' financial reporting and concerns about opaque corporate governance have led to Korean equities being undervalued, as the KOSPI (The Korea Composite Stock Price Index) was found to have a forward price-to-earnings ratio of under ten, or below most other Asian stock markets (Noland, 2013; The Economist, 2012).

Since these two crises, it has become clear that the *chaebol* must navigate a changed corporate governance landscape and respond to new interpretations of business ethics emerging in a mature democracy and global capitalist environment. Such navigation will be particularly challenging in the context of attempts to manage the tradeoffs inherent in attempts to both professionalize management practices while also trying to hang on to past practices. This is seen mostly clearly with regard to attempts to maintain family ownership by handing down ownership from father to son.

5.6 THE SON ALSO RISES: SUCCESSION PLANNING IN THE AGE OF THE EMERGING MARKET AND ENTREPRENEURIAL MODES OF EXCHANGE

In postwar Korea, comprehensive land reform and the rapid expansion of a widely accessible education system (that incorporated merit-based examination systems) have delivered a relatively high degree of social mobility. For many Koreans, intelligence and motivation have been enough to secure career success (Park, 2003). However, they have rarely been enough

to secure the top job of running a *chaebol*. In Korea's *chaebols*, blood has always been thicker than water, and succession of *chaebol* ownership has typically been passed on to the eldest son or the favored heir. In addition to implications for corporate governance standards and the quality of top management, this also has implications for the *chaebol*'s ethical standing in Korean society.

Despite significant corporate governance reforms, it is the issue of succession that will pose the greatest challenge to realizing corporate governance reform and the embedding of a professional managerial culture. While the new "deemed inheritance tax" of more than 50% might impede the ability of families to retain control over their respective *chaebols*, many owner-managers may resort to a variety of irregularity to transfer wealth and management control to their children. In particular, related-party transactions among member firms that favor subsidiaries in which the heir holds a significant equity stake, a form of so-called "tunneling," have been the preferred route for many owner-managers to transfer ownership within the family (Hwang & Kim, 2014; Jung, 2004).[2]

An obvious deficiency of the family succession model is that new owners are not appointed on the basis of verified managerial talent. A lack of talent at the very top is compounded by issues affecting the next tier of management. Korean management teams' performance is rarely tied to the performance of the conglomerate (e.g., it is not tied to the performance of a company's share price). Also, often postsuccession, more experienced senior managers are replaced with those loyal to the new heir. Given such career uncertainty, professional managers have limited incentives to pursue higher returns for the company. Instead, senior managers in a *chaebol* might be tempted to focus on how best to focus on their own financial futures before their probable discharge from the firm (Lee, 1999).

---

[2]Typically, *chaebol* owner-managers hold on to only a very small portion of equities in their listed companies. However, they control the interrelationships between a web of cross-shareholdings across numerous diversified subsidiaries (in 2012 there were 1565 affiliates controlled by 43 *chaebols*). This has allowed owner-managers to extract profits through related-party transactions among member firms -"tunneling," and also extended their control over the whole conglomerate, while removing any mechanism for control from minority shareholders (Jung, 2004). This type of governance may magnify the agency problems and sometimes may hurt the value of the public shareholdings (hence the notion of the "the Korea Discount" discussed above). As part of the reforms after the 1997–98 Asian economic crisis, the government introduced a law targeting cross-shareholdings by placing a limit of 3% of the voting power per shareholder (Jung, 2004).

Succession by the next generation can compromise *chaebols* in other ways, such as their capacity to respond strategically to challenging economic conditions. *Chaebols* run the risk that the second generation can be viewed as less legitimate which, in turn, may encourage the heir to compensate by attempting to achieve something new and different, in effect to prove that they are as capable as their father. According to Lee (1999), such a mentality leads to "careless expansion into new business areas, which often puts the whole group into jeopardy" (p. 20).

In times of economic crisis, control by the anointed son can make adopting and implementing strategic responses even more difficult. While the crisis of 1997 was triggered by a liquidity shortage in the foreign exchange market, the pattern of corporate collapses also suggests that Korea's economic problems at that time has deeper roots in poor managerial practices of many *chaebols*. Between 1996 and 1998, about one-half of the top thirty *chaebols* went bankrupt or were on the brink of bankruptcy, the result of a range of internal and external factors. However, it is interesting to note how many of those *chaebols* that collapsed had recently experienced a succession of ownership from founder to son. According to Lee (1999), in many cases of *chaebol* bankruptcies, one of the most important causes for decline had to do with incorrect strategic decisions made by the new heir. Out of the 24 *chaebols* that went bankrupt at the time of the Asian financial crisis, 14 bankruptcies occurred soon after the descendent of the founder inherited the company (Lee, 1999).

Recent reports suggest that irregularities relating to founders' efforts to pass ownership onto their sons are likely to be more common in the coming years, as wealth transfer is taking place amid tighter controls. Manager-owners must now find ways around tougher anticross-shareholding laws while avoiding large inheritance taxes (e.g., according to some reports, the heirs to the Samsung empire might face an inheritance tax bill of as much as US$6 billion Lee, 2014). Such behavior is also likely to ignite a new round of contestation from civic groups and shareholder activists amid waning support in Korea for conglomerates controlled through crossholdings (Lee, 2014).

5.7 CONCLUSION

In the period between 1953 and the late 1990s, there was no linear or clearly staged trajectory from one mode of exchange to another. Instead, features of manorial, mercantile and, more recently, market and entrepreneurial modes

have coexisted. The coexistence of different modes of exchange has implications for the social construction of business ethics. In the context of mixed modes, how ethics are applied to the behavior of political and economic elites are more fluid. This uncertainty has provided elites with the opportunity to rationalize and justify business practices. In Korea, social and political elites supported each other in their attempts to justify certain practices as acceptable, because they contributed to delivering high economic growth, and normal, because they had roots in Korean cultural tradition. However, the 1997 Asian financial crisis unleashed forces that drove a significant shift in the mode of exchange from manorial/mercantile to a more open and global trade environment. This has created new challenges for the *chaebol*; while professionalism and meritocracy are making some inroads, many *chaebol* owners are struggling to maintain family control.

Thus in the Korean case, business ethics has been linked to modes of exchange that have moved back and forth during the course of its postwar transformation. Korea's political and economic elites have driven this process as they have sought to strategically use hand-crafted business ethics narratives to neutralize opposition to planned transformation of the modes of exchange and pressure for governance reform from within civil society. But with the shift to a market or entrepreneurial mode of exchange, the crafting of business ethics narratives can accommodate *chaebol* manorial or mercantilist behaviors, such that family succession will become increasingly difficult. The ethics of maintaining family ownership has become a difficult message to sell in a mature democracy, active civil society, and globalized economy, and can be further explored within business ethics and the modes of exchange framework.

REFERENCES

Asian Corporate Governance Association Korea. (2012). *CG watch 2012: Tremors and cracks*. http://www.acga-asia.org/public/files/CG_Watch_2012_ACGA_Market_Rankings.pdf.

Berger, P., & Luckmann, T. (1966). *The social construction of reality—A treatise in the sociology of knowledge*. London: Penguin.

Brandt, V. A. (1971). *Korean village between farm and sea*. Cambridge, MA: Harvard University Press.

Chang, S.-J. (2003). *Financial crisis and transformation of Korean business groups: The rise and fall of chaebols*. New York: Cambridge University Press.

Choi, J. J. (1993). Political cleavages in South Korea. In H. Koo (Ed.), *State and society in contemporary Korea*. Ithaca, NY: Cornell University Press.

Clifford, M. (1997). *Troubled tiger* (rev. ed.). Singapore: Butterworth-Heinemann Asia.

Derichs, C., & Heberer, T. (2002). Asian crisis and political change: discourses on political reform in east and southeast Asia. *European Journal of East Asian Studies*, 1(2).

Deuchler, M. (1992). *The confucian transformation of korea: A study of society and ideology*. Cambridge: Council of East Asian Studies, Harvard University.

Eckert, C. (1993). The South Korean bourgeoisie: A class in search of hegemony. In H. Koo (Ed.), *State and society in contemporary Korea*. Ithaca, NY: Cornell University Press.

Faure, G. (2002). Reform and deregulation policies in post-crisis east Asia: An overview of the east Asian reforms. *European Journal of East Asian Studies*, 1(2).

Governance Metrics International. (2010). *Corporate governance ranking, GMI (2010)*. http://www.gmiratings.com/Images/GMI_Country_Rankings_as_of_10_27_2010.pdf.

Hao, Y., & Johnston, M. (1995). China's surge of corruption. *Journal of Democracy*, 6(4).

Hazlehurst, J. (2013). Chaebols: Kings of the conglomerates. *Campden FB*, (56). 25 February 2013. http://www.campdenfb.com/article/chaebols-kings-conglomerates.

Hwang, S., & Kim, W. (2014). *When heirs become major shareholders: Evidence on tunneling and succession through related-party transactions*. ECGI-Finance Working Paper No. 413/2014.

Janelli, R. L., & Janelli, D.Y. (1997). The mutual constitution of Confucianism and capitalism in South Korea. In T. Brook & H.V. Luong (Eds.), *Culture and economy: The shaping of capitalism in Eastern Asia*. Ann Arbor, MI: University of Michigan Press.

Janelli, R. L., & Yim, D. (1993). *Making capitalism: The social and cultural construction of a South Korean conglomerate*. Stanford, CA: Stanford University Press.

Jeong, J. (1986). *I achimedo seolleimeul ango [Feeling the thrill again this morning]*. Seoul: Samseong Chulpansa.

Jung, D.-H. (2004). Korean chaebol in transition. *China Report*, 40(3), 299–303.

Kim, H., Hoskisson, R. E., Tihanyi, L., & Hong, J. (2004). The evolution and restructuring of diversified business groups in emerging markets: The lessons from chaebols in Korea. *Asia Pacific Journal of Managemen*, 21(1–2).

Kirk, D. (2014). Obsessed with control, some Korean tycoons end up in handcuffs. *Forbes*, (Forbes April 30 2014).

Lee, K. (1999). *Corporate governance and growth in the Korean chaebols: A microeconomic foundation for the 1997 crisis*. Seoul: Seoul National University.

Lee, J. (2014). Samsung family struggles to keep grip on most powerful chaebo. *The Washington Post*, (July 23, 2014).

Lie, J. 1992a. The concept of mode of exchange. *American Sociological Review*, 57(4).

Lie, J. 1992b. The political economy of South Korean development. *International Sociology*, 7(3).

Noland, M. (2013). Six markets to watch: South Korea. *Foreign Affairs*, 6.

Oh, I., & Varcin, R. (2002). The mafioso state: Stateled market bypassing in South Korea and Turkey. *Third World Quarterly*, 23(4).

Palais, J. B. (1996). *Confucian statecraft and Korean institutions: Yu Hyongwon and the Late Choson Dynasty*. Seattle, WA: University of Washington.

Park, H. (2003). Intergenerational social mobility among Korean men in comparative perspective. *Research in Social Stratification and Mobility*, 20.

Pontell, H. N., & Geis, G. L. (2010). Introduction: White-collar and corporate crime in Asia. *Asian Journal of Criminology*, 5(2).

Reed, D. (2002). Corporate governance reforms in developing countries. *Journal of Business Ethics*, 37.

Robinson, M. (1991). Perceptions of confucianism in twentieth century Korea. In G. Rozman (Ed.), *The East Asian region: Confucian heritage and its modern adaptation*. Princeton, NJ: Princeton University Press.

Shim, J. H. (1992a). Caught by the system. *Far Eastern Economic Review*.

Shim, J. H. (1992b). Mr. Clean comes clean. *Far Eastern Economic Review*.

Suh, J., & Chen, D. H. C. (2007). *Korea as a knowledge economy: Evolutionary process and lessons learned*. In J. Suh & D. H. C. Chen (Eds.), Washington, DC: Korea Development Institute and The World Bank Institute.

The Economist. (2012). *The Korea discount: corporate governance explains South Korea's low stock-market ratings* (11 February 2012). http://www.economist.com/node/21547255.

Trivellato, B. (2002). Corporate and financial sector reform in the wake of the Asian crisis: Malaysia and Thailand. *European Journal of East Asian Studies, 1*(2).

Williams, R. (1977). *Marxism and literature*. Oxford: OUP.

Yun, J.-W. (2010). The myth of confucian capitalism in South Korea: Overworked elderly and underworked youth. *Pacific Affairs, 83*(2).

CHAPTER 6

Mapping K-Pop Past and Present: Shifting the Modes of Exchange

K. Howard
SOAS, University of London, London, United Kingdom

6.1 WHAT EXACTLY IS THE RECORDED MUSIC INDUSTRY?

How can the K-pop music industry be theorized, and how well does it fit conventional accounts of the global music industry? The global industry is typically regarded as a recorded music industry that embraces and controls the creativity of artists while simultaneously seeking to influence the tastes of consumers in order to generate profits. In other words, it finds and contracts artists through talent scouts, agents and managers, and producers and sound engineers, and it controls the recorded products that it then promotes and distributes. At both ends of the operation, artists and retailers lament their small share of the total revenue; they claim to be caught by an efficient industrial juggernaut.

Within the recorded music industry, relationships between today's three "majors" (Universal, Sony, and Warner) and "independents" or "indies" are constantly negotiated. Fans want artists to resist the majors which they claim limit creativity (consider the mainstreaming of Korean punk with Crying Nut's 2002 Soccer World Cup Anthem "*O p'ilsŭng k'oria*/Victory, Korea" (Jave/Universal DK0302, 2002)). Commentators celebrate individual artists or groups, while others adopt a critical approach (e.g., Adorno and Horkheimer (1972), Chapple and Garofalo (1977), Harker (1980), and Manuel (1988)), holding that the music industry is an "assembly line" based on "premasticated formulae" that "colonizes leisure". In contrast, the International Federation of Phonographic Industries (IFPI) issues annual reports that spin the music industry as one of today's great global industries, in which independent and multinational production companies underpin the livelihoods of thousands of artists across the world. To IFPI, revenues accrue from sales of recordings and as a consequence pressure is applied to state authorities to enhance copyright protection. Hence, in respect to the Korean industry:

> *The value of the South Korean recorded music market increased from $148.5 million in 2008 to $195 million in 2011… One of the key rewards of South Korea's improved legal environment is more investment in local artists… The government began to update its copyright law in 2007…usage of cyberlockers fell by 38% in 2012 and, according to authorities, 70% of cyberlocker users [now] stop infringing after receiving their first notice (http://www.ifpi.org/south-korea.php).*[1]

IFPI conveniently overlooks history. In 2002, Korea was the second-largest music market in Asia, with a domestic turnover of $300 million (*Time*, 29 July, 2002); SM Entertainment, listed on Korea's KOSDAQ stock market, then controlled around 70 stars, amongst them H.O.T. who, starting in 1996, shifted ten million albums in their five-year existence, and whose fan base survived beyond their demise, particularly in China (Pease, 2006, pp. 176–189). Such figures seem unimaginable today: sales of recordings fell by over 20% year-on-year between 2002 and 2005, and only seven albums sold more than 100,000 copies in 2004.

IFPI's market model assumes a social organization of commodity exchange that hardly matches Korea, and is unrepresentative of markets in the Global South. Broadly stated, only in the 1990s did Korea see anything resembling the conventional market model operating for K-pop. From its early days until then, partnerships between a controlling government and a set of local or regional recording companies and broadcasters, mediated by an army of fixers, limited both the size and profits of the market. More recently, the emergence of transnational entertainment companies has reasserted control over artists; companies have forged partnerships both with a government keen to promote Korean "soft culture" abroad but unwilling to censor the profit-generating industry, and with a range of commercial enterprises. The latter utilize K-pop to promote their own products, along the lines of Oh and Park's (2012) supply chain model: the music industry now produces products that serve other industries (B2B), but generate little directly from sales to consumers (B2C). Psy's eminently mashable "Gangnam Style" neatly illustrates: people around the world were invited to freely produce parodies, without paying any fees:

> *It is the cringe-proof meme, the zombie meme, the meme that knows no shame. Quite possibly, it will be danced by grannies at weddings in 2030–the 21st-century equivalent of the conga line; the new macarena. (Patrick Kingsley, at http://www.theguardian.com/music/shortcuts/2012/nov/14/can-anyone-kill-gangnam-style)*

---

[1] All websites last accessed 2 May, 2016.

Korea's entertainment companies have leap-frogged the global music industry, reducing the importance of recordings as physical objects. The rest of the world is playing catch-up, as Gideon Spanier's discussion of Scooter Braun, who signed Psy as "Gangnam Style" took off in 2012, tellingly reveals:

> Braun's company, Scooter Braun Projects, may manage music artists, but traditional recorded music from downloads and CDs is almost the least of his priorities. 'It's not even on artists' minds', declares Braun… Instead it's all about touring, merchandising and other opportunities such as branding, sponsorship, and sync [rights] ('Scooter is a Belieber in music to build brands', Evening Standard 25 June 2014).

A new model is needed, and John Lie's modes of exchange offer utility. Modes of exchange map the music industry as it emerged in Korea as a largely closed trade commercialization based on social relations and power that with the coming of democracy in the early 1990s, briefly blossomed as an open market, before coalescing into today's transregional mercantile virtual monopoly supported by state policies to enhance growth. In its colonial (up to 1945) and postcolonial (1945–1992) phases, control was embedded within shared social discourses of ethics and morality, and top-down political censorship. Control was, at times, challenged by artists and consumers, generating underground music scenes. However, in the 1990s, as the newly democratized government abrogated responsibility for policing morality, so the emerging entrepreneurial entertainment companies imposed their own control agendas, targeting new audiences at home and abroad.

6.2 THE COLONIAL PERIOD TO 1945: THE KOREAN MUSIC INDUSTRY, AND ITS CENSORSHIP MECHANISMS, EMERGES

The recorded music industry treats sound as an autonomous object. Such a notion predates the invention of the phonograph in 1877—the device that largely enabled it to become normative. Early recordings encouraged sales of machines on which to play them. The earliest recordings were of speech, and the first known music recordings, in 1887, featured the pianist Josef Hofmann performing in Thomas Alvin Edison's laboratory at Newark. Twelve years later, an advert published in the Korean *Hwangsŏng Sinmun* newspaper on 13 March, 1989 marks the first known reference to music recordings for sale in Korea (reproduced in No, 1995, p. 657). These were of Western music. Adverts continued to promote machines over recordings for the next decade, as European and American engineers began a process

of making local recordings in and for specific territories. Fred Gaisberg (1983–1951) visited China and Japan in 1903, to, as he later put it, "open up new markets, establish agencies, and acquire a catalog of native records" (Gaisberg, 1942, p. 48).[2] His recordings of Chinese and Japanese music, pressed in the Old World, were distributed in Asia via local Victor agents (Gronow, 1981). The German Beka-Record company sent an expedition to China and Japan in 1905, advertising its resulting catalog to local dealers in 1906 (Bumb, 1976), the year now considered to mark the publication of the first recordings made in Korea, recorded in November, attributed to Gaisberg and the Columbia Graphophone Company, and again distributed through Victor. The American F.W. Horne had been one of the first to retail gramophones and recordings in Japan shortly before the beginning of the century and by 1910 Japan had its first home-grown recorded music company, Nipponophone (Nippon Chikuonki Shōkai). Curiously, East Asia tends to be conspicuously absent from accounts of the development of the recording industry (see, e.g., Day, 2002), but we know that an agreement confined European and American companies to China and left Japanese territories a monopoly of Japanese companies. Hence, Korea, controlled by Japan from this time to 1945, "served as a major arena where the Japanese recording industry embarked on an imperialist undertaking" (Yamauchi, 2012, pp. 146–147).

The extent to which Japanese recording companies could make profits in Korea reflected the distribution of gramophones. As expensive commodities, these machines were initially the preserve of a largely Japanese elite. Trade in recordings involved limited participation, within what Lie would characterize as a manorial mode (1992, pp. 513–514). By the late 1920s, however, when recording studios were still concentrated in Japan and disk pressing was still all done in Japan (and as continued to be the case into the 1940s: Hwang, 1989, pp. 151–181; Pak, 2009), six Japanese companies had established Korean subsidiaries: Columbia, Victor, Polydor, Teichuku, Taihei, and Chieron, with Teichuku allied to Okeh for the Korean market and Taihei to T'aep'yŏng. Korean scholars argue about the nature of the relationships and focus on the localized (Korean) industry (see, e.g., Chang, 2006): trade had clearly spread among the colonized, and had led to increased recording

---

[2]The first known recordings of Korean music had actually been made in 1896 by Alice Cunningham Fletcher in Washington DC, featuring three young Koreans. Stored in the Library of Congress, these have been released on CD in Korea by Chŏng Ch'anggwan (CKJCD-010, 2007).

production targeting Koreans.[3] Within Lie's formulation, trade in recordings was moving towards a mercantile mode, and this was perceived by the colonial government to require monitoring. New control mechanisms were needed, since legislation relating to copyright had from the 1710 British Statute of Anne onwards been concerned with printed materials. As a result, the fixing of sound as a physical entity initially tended to require printed notations or lyric sheets. Censors needed a tangible object to assess, and found it in printed materials. Policing recordings applied the existing publication law until 1933, when a separate ordinance was put in place in Korea to govern the new-fangled technology. This still considered that notes and printed song texts could satisfy inspection requirements, but a revision to the Japanese equivalent law made in 1934 in Tokyo began to expect the submission of recordings.[4] Still, as the censors judged songs unacceptably nostalgic, disturbing, degenerative, or pornographic, printed texts initially remained more important. Over time judgments came to reflect music and singing as well, and the archives reveal increasingly frequent references to "*kachō*" (J., song + melody) (Yamauchi, 2011, pp. 93–99).

The censorship operated haphazardly, in that some Korean recordings were banned but others were not. This was the case with "*Arirang*," of which multiple recordings were made (Atkins, 2007). Although colonial censorship is recalled negatively by a number of Korean scholars (e.g., Yi, 1984, pp. 83–119, 2000), a reinterpretation is needed. Why would Japanese recording companies, or companies controlled by Japanese businessmen that were concerned primarily with making profit, want to challenge the authorities that governed Korea? Mercantile elites, Lie tells us citing Fernand Braudel, tend to be connected to central political authorities in relationships that help police trade (1992, p. 514).

Looking more closely at the developing Korean music industry in the 1930s, a further mode of exchange is observable, Lie's entrepreneurial mode: "entrepreneurial traders are essentially simple commodity traders connecting producers to consumers or other producers beyond their region" (1992, pp. 514–515). With this in mind, the emergence of the Korean

---

[3]The operation of Japanese labels in Korea is pursued in Yamauchi's doctoral dissertation (2009a). Kim (2000b), Pae (2011), and the annual volumes of *Han'guk ŭmbanhak* (Korean Discology; 1991–) offer extensive analyses of recordings issued in Korea during the colonial period.

[4]As the collection of recordings grew, discussions began about setting up a library of recorded sound (Yamauchi, 2011, pp. 89 and 112); Japan considered following France, which instituted a law on the legal deposit of recordings in 1925 (Day, 2002, p. 232).

music industry mirrors the development of Japanese industry after the collapse of Tokugawa in 1867, and also matches accounts of the establishment of Korea's future conglomerates during the colonial period. It developed with a corpus of fixers. By the 1920s, fixers connected Japanese companies to local Korean artists and consumers, facilitating both ends of the industry—from talent scouting to artist management,[5] from engaging instrumental backing musicians to sourcing repertory, and from travel (since, until the 1930s, Korean artists traveled to Japan to record) to studio management (Pak, 2009). Fixers handled much of the promotion of both artists and recordings, including to the increasingly important radio stations and newspapers. Recognizing their importance, Japanese companies by the 1930s employed Koreans directly, typically in their *Bungeibu* (Literature and Art Departments) (Yamauchi, 2009b, p. 142), by which time Koreans were supplementing officials in the colonial administration.[6]

6.3 POSTLIBERATION, 1945–1992: THE KOREAN MUSIC INDUSTRY REFORMED

The Republic of Korea inherited the existing mechanisms to monitor and control sound recordings. While it recognized the potential of music for propaganda in the run-up to the Korean War, rebuilding the country after 1953 left legislators with more important concerns than dealing with a floundering industry. The recording industry needed to be rebuilt, and this began in earnest when the first domestic LP pressing plant opened in 1962. Albums, not singles, became the industry staple: singles were costly to tool and produce. It was 1962, though, when Park Chung Hee's authoritarian regime consolidated its power, and a raft of legislation was soon put in place. Control was initially vested in the Korean Broadcasting Review Committee (Han'guk pangsong simŭi wiwŏnhoe) and from 1975 onwards, in the Korean Public Performances Screening Committee (Han'guk kongyŏn yulli wiwŏnhoe). Between 1965 and 1975, 223 Korean songs and 261 Western songs were banned (Shin and Kim, 2014, p. 285), starting with Cho Myŏngam's "*Kiro ŭi hwanghon*/Crossroads in the twilight": Cho, along

---

[5]A number of Korean artists were promoted on Japanese recordings, often taking Japanese identities. This fascinating aspect of the colonial period is discussed by Yamauchi (2012, pp. 152–164) in terms of embracing musical others and embodying cultural difference. It might also be considered in terms of "glocalization" and its counterpart, "reterritorialization" (after Iwabuchi (2002) and Tomlinson (2003)).

[6]Yamauchi (2009a) cites relevant archived documents from the period.

with many left-leaning artists in the immediate postliberation years, had settled in the Democratic People's Republic of Korea, and so any song by him was considered to threaten national security. Again, negative memories of colonialism meant that songs with a perceived Japanese flavor (*waesaek*) were soon banned. These included, most famously, Yi Mija's "*Tongbaek agassi*/The Camellia Girl." When this and two of her other songs were banned, she is reported to have contemplated suicide (Yi, 2004, p. 25). Quite what was meant by Japanese flavor long remained a subject for debate (Pak, 2006, pp. 62–71).

Western songs were scrutinized, often coopting resident foreigners for help: Paul Simon's "Cecilia" fell foul in 1973 for being miserable, "House of the Rising Sun" was found too depressing in 1975, and Bob Dylan's "Blowing in the Wind" was deemed to promote unacceptable pacifism (Han'guk pangsong simŭi wiwŏnhoe, 1981, pp. 95, 125; see also Hwang, 2006). Some songs were banned not for lyrics or music: the collage on the cover of The Beatles' album *Sgt. Peppers' Lonely Heart Club Band*, for example, contained an unacceptable postage-stamp sized portrait of Karl Marx. Expanding control marked Park's administration and by September 1981, 787 Korean songs and 659 Western songs had been banned (Kim, 2000a, p. 411). Amongst these, Queen's "Bohemian Rhapsody" had unacceptably violent lyrics, but once banned it became a favorite bootleg (Kang, 1999). Roald Maliangkay outlines a number of reasons for censoring songs: corrupting lyrics (*t'oep'yejŏgin kasa*), defeatism (*p'aebae*), masochism (*chahakchŏk*), and national security (*kukka anbo*) (2006b, p. 51). Additional reasons given by the "group sound" founder, Shin Joong Hyun, who had more songs than anybody else banned, included vulgar lyrics (*kasa chŏsok*), immature singing (*ch'angbŏp misuk*), and aggravating mistrust and cynicism (*pulsin p'ungt'o chojang*) (Shin and Kim, 2014, pp. 295–296).

The Korean media self-censored, and domestic recording companies needing approval from government organs were careful not to release anything that might attract government ire. One result was that Shin's group sound came to operate primarily as underground music. Although celebrated today, not least by those who were part of that underground, group sound (and by the 1980s, heavy metal) was not mainstream pop prior to 1992. The mainstream consisted predominantly of ballads about love (but, to keep on the right side of the censor, omitting anything that might be considered vulgar or corrupting). Consider Cho Yong Pil's cover of "Bohemian Rhapsody," "*Koch'u chamjari*/Red Dragonfly" (Seoul Records SRCD-3185, 1992). While Cho keeps Queen's binary musical structure, alternating short

punchy phrases with lyrical sections, the lyrics ("Mother, I just killed a man/put a gun against his head…") are completely absent:

> Maybe I'm still immature. That might be it. Mother! Why do I keep waiting? Mother! Why do I suddenly miss them?
> When I look at the sky with a heart moist with loneliness I'm dizzy. Dizzy whizzy like a red dragonfly flying away.

Again, the major disco hit of 1992 was Lee Hyun Woo's "*Kkum*/Dream":

> And when I close my eyes, memories of yesterday come to me like a dream.
> Deep inside my heart I know that you're the only one I truly loved.
> I gave you all my heart and soul, don't you know it's true? (Sinsegye SISCD-115, 1992).

Lee's "Dream" was recorded in 1990, but was not released: it contained rap, something not permitted. All this changed in 1992, when Seo Taiji and Boys debuted. Seo introduced rap to the public, but initially, similarly kept his lyrics within what the censor would allow.

Challenging the market was never easy. Back in the 1960s, bands successful at serving the needs of American forces stationed in Korea struggled to sell to domestic consumers. Many artists honed their skills working for the American Eighth Army, hired because they were cheaper than American singers. Some, such as The Kim Sisters, went on to have success in America (Maliangkay, 2006a, pp. 27–30; Shin and Kim, 2014, pp. 277–280). When Add Four's first album was released in Seoul in 1964, Shin Joong Hyun recalls that record stores "were returning the unsold copies en masse no later than a week after release" (cited in Lee, 2007, p. 61). Shin, however, had a second career, as impresario, introducing "The Pearl Sisters" and others to the market. The local industry remained small, even though mercantile in orientation. Partly, this reflected censorship, but also, government rules forbade foreign music companies operating in Korea. The media profiling of pop created an even greater challenge, since it poorly matched youth interests, opening a chasm between radio charts and sales figures. As Byeon Jin Seop's "*Hŭimang sahang*/Wish List," a song that peaked at Number 5 in the Music Box charts on 9 February, 1990 then quickly fell away, illustrates, since although it never generated a fan base among the youth it was endlessly played on the media.

While fixers facilitated both ends of the industry, their entrepreneurship now primarily served the media. Their identity changed as they aligned themselves with what became known as—in Korea as in Japan—the "star system" (discussed by the former MBC producer Yi (1996: particularly,

pp. 247–253 and 269–286)). Contests such as campus song festivals encouraged fresh-faced amateur singers to present new material; compilation albums were produced, and scouts signed new talent both for the music industry and for potential media careers. The male singer, actor, and film composer Kim Soochul, for example, won top prize at the 1978 University Music Festival leading his combo, Little Big Man. Two albums and three solo hits led to Lee being voted 1984's top singer by both major broadcasters, KBS and MBC. He was commissioned to contribute music to the 1986 Asian Games and the 1988 Seoul Olympics (and, later, the 2002 FIFA World Cup). Again, the female singer Lee Sun-Hee won the grand prize at the First Riverside Song Festival in 1984. She completed eight albums by 1992, by which time a political career beckoned as she stood as a government candidate in Seoul's Map'o ward.

Once established, stars typically worked with songs created by others—lyricists, composers, and arrangers. This was made normative by the major broadcasters, who employed resident backing bands, music arrangers, and conductors, as well as dance groups and choreographers. At the same time, the media annexed the identity of songs through faux talent shows in which the public demonstrated (questionable) singing skills. The result was that songs became hits less for individual singers than because they were widely sung. Media play, then, whether by an original singer or of covers, became more important than album sales. As a result, the mercantile mode folded back into a manorial mode. The recording industry remained, through the 1980s, a cottage industry, playing second fiddle to broadcasting as public service. The system was maintained not least because copyright was limited: although Korea revised its laws to align them with the Universal Copyright Convention in 1986, an exception continued to allow the production of compilation albums featuring hits. Songs released a minimum of 18 months earlier could be freely used, providing their inclusion on the compilation was registered with, and fixed fees were paid to the Korea Music Copyright Association (KOMCA). Compilations using this exception continued into the new century with "trot medleys" (Son, 2006, pp. 77–81).

6.4 1992: EXPLODING BALLADS

Seo Taiji and Boys burst onto Korean TV screens in Mar. 1992. Koreans encountered rap, and four of the band's tracks held sway in the music charts during the year. Their first album notched up 1.5 million sales and their next three added two million more (Kim, 2000a, p. 245).

Seo (real name Chŏng Hyŏnch'ŏl, b.1972) introduced a new concept of star based on image: an image controlled by artists rather than the company suits of the music industry and the media, an image that had no place for studio bands, backing dancers, or the hierarchy of lyricists, arrangers, and composers. The image was formed by costume (Kim, 2000a, p. 245), prototypical b-boy dance (Maliangkay, 2014, p. 300), and rap. A veritable explosion of pop followed as more foreign styles were appropriated: reggae became hip hop starting with Kim Gun Mo's "*P'inggye*/Excuse" (Dukyun DYCD-7016, 1993), interpretations of house and rave started with Noise (Dukyun DYCD-7011, 1993), rap met reggae in Roo'ra's "Roots of Reggae" (Daewoo DWP CP-0007, 1994), and a strangely literal interpretation of jungle arrived with Park Mi Kyung's "*Ebŭi ŭi kyŏnggo*/Eve's Warning" (Line LC-1002, 1995). The introduction of heavy metal heard on Seo's third album (Bando BDCD-023, 1994) had long been part of the underground with groups such as Sinawe (Seo had played bass on Sinawe's fourth album), Puhwal and Baekdoosan, and morphed into the mainstream not least with Shin Hae Chul's N.EX.T's (New Experimental Team) album *Home* (Jigu JCDS-0317, 1992).

Popular participation in the rapidly emerging market transformed the music industry into a social organization of open trade, much as Lie explains how as particular groups gain control over the means of exchange they construct a new mode of exchange (1992, p. 512). One way to theorize what Seo Taiji and Boys achieved is to cite Appadurai's (1990, pp. 1–14) concepts of "ideoscapes" and "technoscapes," and to frame these within a notion of deterritorialization brought by the increasing familiarity with globalized cultural forms. Certainly, with satellite broadcasting, demand grew for visual imaging, rather than just audio soundtracks. This arrived in Hong Kong with billionaire Li Ka Shing's Star TV in 1990 and spread across Asia through Star TV's tie-up with MTV. In geographically contained Korea, cable TV was equally important, with the nation's first cable music channel, M-Net, being founded in 1993. Music videos were needed, and "Excuse" is remembered as having Korea's first.

An alternative theorization would see in the explosion of pop the cultural expression of a new generation, the *sinsedae*. This generation, born in the 1970s, had no memory of the Korean War and its aftermath. Its culture replaced the student-led song movement and culture-of-the-masses of the 1970s and 1980s with an individualism that challenged social norms (Kwon, 2014; Maliangkay, 2014). The *sinsedae* came of age at a time of democratization when, after three decades of military control and with the successful

hosting of the 1988 Seoul Olympic Games functioning as a coming-of-age, Koreans were determined to make the most of new-found freedoms. They embraced the world outside and challenged the internal cultural economy. Suddenly, the music industry looked much more like the industry image that IFPI continues to promote. The *sinsedae* was familiar with American popular culture, and Seo's songs were influenced by American pop (Jung, 2006, pp. 113–114, 118). The lack of international majors operating in Korea made for a permissive culture, hence accusations of borrowing were frequent. "*Chŏnsang yusae*" on Roo'ra's third album (World Music WMCD-1023, 1996) controversially sampled a Japanese track "*Omatsuri Ninja*," while Shinwha's second album, *T.O.P.* was considered to be heavily indebted to the American group Lacrosse. Appropriating foreign elements created the foundation for claims that K-pop has over time been "de-Koreanized" (Shin, 2009, pp. 513–515) and become "culturally odorless" (Jung, 2011, p. 3), "too white" (Hübinette, 2012, p. 523) and "trapped" as a hybrid form between the national and the global (Cho, 2011, p. 388).

When Seo took aim at the frenetic cramming of the education system in his 2004 rap-metal "*Kyosil Idea/*Classroom Ideology," the media banned the song. Undeterred, in 1995 he sang about the alienation of youth under strict parental control in the gangsta rap "Come Back Home" (Bando BDCD-028, 1995). The old forms of censorship and control had become obsolete. Control, however, was never abandoned, but shifted from music and lyrics to image. Seo band's dreadlocks led to television bans, perhaps linked to the notion of rap and reggae as resistance (Maliangkay, 2014, p. 301, citing Kim, 2001, pp. 129–130). And, by 1997, KBS television banned male pop stars having earrings, dyed hair, tattoos, or exposing their navels (*Korea Newsreview*, 19 July, 1997, p. 32), while female stars were expected to be cute (*aegyo*) but never in-your-face sexy.

6.5 PACKAGING KOREAN POP, 1996 ONWARDS

The charisma of Seo had, in a Weberian way, been routinized: Korean pop became visual as much as aural, and danced as much as sung. This facilitated its packaging by new entrepreneurs in the form of entertainment companies. The first was Lee Soo Man's SM Entertainment. Lee (b.1952) recalls how, as a student, he gathered with others to listen to pop from abroad and local guitar songs at downtown Seoul venues such as Green Frog Hall (*Ch'ŏng kaeguri hol*) and C'est si bon (*Sesibong*), then aligned himself to the song movement (An and Kong, 2012, pp. 51–62, 119–28). He formed

SM Entertainment in 1993, but it was his made-to-measure group H.O.T. (High Five of Teenagers) that created what his biographers term a "success museum" or "success music". Lee reflected on how the media had sourced stars in song contests, and how key musicians and promoters helped form successful groups. He advertised auditions, recruiting H.O.T.'s first three members. The fourth was chosen after casting calls in front of the youngsters the group would target in Seoul, and the fifth was recruited in Los Angeles (along with a putative sixth member, Andy Lee, who ended up signing with another SM band, Shinwha). Recognizing that visuals were as important as music, he tested dance as much as vocal skills (An and Kong, 2012, pp. 280–302).

H.O.T. became the model for other entertainment companies, including, to complete the triumvirate of the largest of today's more than 30 companies, JYP Entertainment and YG Entertainment. Where SM had a market capitalization of 780 billion *wŏn* in 2013, YG Entertainment, founded in 1996 and taking its name from the initials of the nickname of its founder Yang Hyŏnsŏk, had a capitalization of 515 billion *wŏn*, and JYP, founded in 1997 and taking its name from the initials of its founder, Jin-Young Park, 120 billion *wŏn* (*The Economist*, 26 October, 2013). Each fuses together the different elements of the music industry, absorbing fixers into the company, each functioning as talent agencies that scout, recruit, train, dress, and control singers, production agencies who control composers, lyricists, arrangers, set designers and film crew, and promotion agencies to the media selling not just products but also product placements for others. The companies were not exempt from suffering as sales of recorded music collapsed, and it is only in recent years that B2B revenue streams have become profitable. Indeed, according to the *Sŏul Sinmun* (4 April, 2012), SM Entertainment made annual losses of between 1.2 billion and 3.7 billion *wŏn* between 2003 and 2008, but from 2009 on it reported annual profits on rising sales that in 2011 brought 20.3 billion *wŏn* in profits on sales of 109 billion.

There are two inevitable results of the way entertainment companies operate. The first is the product: "highly produced, sugary boy- and girl-bands with slick dance routines and catchy tunes," as Lucy Williamson wrote for the BBC, or, as MTV's Iggy had it, "bubblegum pop [that] is a very serious, very expensive business" (http://www.bbc.co.uk/news/world-asia- pacific-13760064 and http://www.mtviggy.com/articles/k-pop-un-covered- making-bubblegum-part-1/). Dance choreography is replicable, allowing cover dance memes that create communities of fans—dance trackers (Khiun, 2013)—and social networking sites allow, as with parodies

of "Gangnam Style," private memes that increase public circulation flows (Jung and Hirata, 2012). The second result is restrictive agreements with artists that have been dubbed "slave contracts." Contracts monitor and control, replacing the roles formerly taken by government officials, restricting artists but leaving companies with a free moral compass. When H.O.T. disbanded in 2001, rumors circulated that the reason was the financial terms being imposed in a new contract by SM (http://english.chosun.com/site/data/html_dir/2001/05/14/2001051461431.html), even though two band members, Kangta and Mun Hŭijun, later released further albums under SM. Contracts came under close scrutiny in 2009, when three members of TVXQ (Dong Bang Shin Ki), took SM to court, citing their 13-year contract as being too long, restrictive, and punitive. The court ruled in their favor, and a subsequent report found that 230 artists with 19 agencies suffered with unlawful contracts. Yoona of Girls Generation was found to be under a 13-year contract, the members of SuperJunior had contracts varying from five to 13-years in duration, and Shinee's members had contracts lasting from six to 13-years.

Internet forums take sides. Most argue that contracts restrict artistry, but some note that the costs of producing a group are high, and must support vocal and dance coaches, stylists, practice venues, accommodation, food, staff payments, and so on. The costs to create a uniform visual image include plastic surgery; formerly largely associated with girl bands, this has become more common among male artists with the metrosexual soft masculinity of the new millennium—as epitomized by Beast.[7] Others argue that restrictive contracts are a necessity given the need to perfect all aspects of presentation: only those prepared to undertake years of training will succeed. The captions to stills from a 2NE1 television feature on the website beyondhallyu.com illustrate: "It's 12 hours before the first TV show, but we don't even have time to sleep"; "We worked too hard"; "I can't wait any longer to get on stage" (http://beyondhallyu.com/k-pop/k-pop-slave-contracts-a-closer-look/). Many internet discussions cite an *Al Jazeera* program broadcast in October 2012 that featured an interview with Joy from RaNia, whose contract permitted no phone, no boyfriends, and limited contact with friends (http://www.aljazeera.com/news/asia-pacific/2012/01/2012126171244109114.html).

---

[7] For a discussion of soft masculinity and the metrosexual male, see Jung (2011, pp. 35–117). Lee (2012, pp. 127–187) offers a discussion of plastic surgery and the Korean Wave.

The website extrakorea cites 2 PM, Girls' Generation and T-ara, and their songs "*10-chŏm manjŏme 10-chŏm/*10 out of 10," "Oh!" and "Bo Peep" (http://extrakorea.wordpress.com/2010/03/25/how-k-pop-trainees-are-mistreated/):

> Every time we record a song, our boss...emphasizes that we should sing very emotionally. During those times, there are specific emotions that he assigns to each of us... To me he said, 'You show anger. You show anger no matter what'.
> The part where the lyrics go 'Oppa, I love you' was really difficult... No matter how much I practiced, when it came time to record, I couldn't sing it...
> When we first received the animal costumes for our first performance, we were really embarrassed and didn't know what to do... There are many who raised their doubts about our style...[but] the truth is all our costumes were ideas of our boss.

Ga-In of Brown Eyed Girls relates how when she first encountered the hip-swaying choreography for "Abracadabra," she was shocked by how racy and sexy it was. She was not sufficiently shocked, though, to refuse reprising the dance for Psy's 2013 "Gentleman," his follow-up to "Gangnam Style," nor to stop her giving an even more explicit performance in "Fxxk U"—a 2014 track about violent love. Similarly explicit videos released in 2014 were Gary's "*Chogŭm itta shawŏhae/*Shower Later" (Gary is one half of the duo LeeSsang) and the YB Band cover of a 1970s song, "Cigarette Girl," both of which threw out the soft masculinity of recent years and featured scantily clad Caucasian lovers. Cutesy has been replaced by overt sexualization: the dollification of female artists—G.Na is 168 cm tall, 47 kg, with natural D-cup breasts—targets an audience, and sits alongside strong female identities promoted in groups such as Miss A, 2NE1, and Brown Eyed Girls. Ga-In's transformation in "Fxxk U" shows how the company decides on her image to target a segmented market. Critics might argue that the government's abandonment of its role as censor has left a moral vacuum in which entertainment companies police themselves but are more concerned with maximizing their profits. And, those restrictions that remain in place are challenged for commercial reasons. Hence, Yonhap News reported on Sep. 20, 2012 how the government conceded to a campaign to lift the 19 rating given to "Right Now," the 2010 title track to Psy's fifth album, because its rating was said to be damaging Psy's ability to emerge as a global superstar following the success of "Gangnam Style."

At the beginning of the new millennium, the Korean government saw export potential in K-pop: popularizing soft culture would lead to consumers buying products such as Samsung and LG phones, TVs and computers, and bring tourists flocking to Korea. A hidden intraregional mercantile

market grew, first teaching Korean stars Mandarin and Japanese, to release Chinese and Japanese versions of songs (Pease, 2006, p. 176), then replacing covers of Japanese songs with Korean songs recast as domestic products in new markets. And, when entertainment companies struggled to market K-pop, the government provided overt and hidden subsidies (Hesmondhalgh, 2013, p. 303; Hong, 2014). To build intraregional trade, they next recruited foreign artists: SM Entertainment's f(x) features two non-Korean members, Californian-born Taiwanese Amber (Amber Liu) and Qingdao-born Victoria (Song Qian); Miss A features two Chinese-born members, Fei (Wang Feifei) from Hainan and Jia (Meng Jia) from Hunan; 2 PM's Nichkhun Horvejkul is an American-born Chinese Thai.

6.6 CONCLUSION

The open, global market of K-pop today comes at a price. Entertainment companies segment and fill markets with songs produced on an "assembly line" based on "premasticated formulae." As they strive for advantage in transregional mercantile activity, they seek to control all aspects of production, thereby constraining the creativity of artists. The censoring government of earlier decades no longer arbitrates, but sponsors and promotes the activities of Korea's soft culture entrepreneurs. The government has, keeping with neo-liberalism as practiced more widely, abrogated moral and ethical responsibility to entertainment companies in the belief that K-pop generates trade in Korea's industrial production. This, though, is not the global or Korean recorded music industry portrayed by the IFPI. At best, the Federation's vision mirrored an industry that in Korea operated for a handful of years in the 1990s. Rather, today's industry looks back on its earlier form—a closed trade commercialization based on social relations and power—learns from the mediatization of the "star system," and spearheads a move into a world in which profit accrues from everything except direct sales of its primary product—recordings.

REFERENCES

Adorno, T. W., & Horkheimer, M. (1972). The culture industry: Enlightenment as mass deception. In G. S. Noerr (Ed.), *Dialectic of Enlightenment* (pp. 94–136). Stanford, CA: Stanford University Press.

An, Y. & Kong, H. (Eds.), (2012). *Yi Suman: Taehan min'guk munhwa sanŏp kaech'ŏkcha-e kwanhan pogosŏ*. Seoul: Chŏngbowa saram.

Appadurai, A. (1990). Disjuncture and difference in the global cultural economy. *Public Culture*, 2, 1–24. Spring.

Atkins, E. (2007). Taylor, The dual career of "Arirang": The Korean resistance anthem that became a Japanese pop hit. *The Journal of Asian Studies*, *66*(3), 645–687.
Bumb, H. (1976). The great beka "Expedition" 1905–6. *The Talking Machine Review*, *41*, 729–733.
Chang, Y. (2006). *Oppanŭn p'unggak chaengiya: Taejung kayoro pon kŭndae ŭi p'unggyŏng*. Seoul: Minŭmsa.
Chapple, S., & Garofalo, R. (1977). *Rock 'n' roll's here to pay: The history and politics of the music industry*. Chicago, IL: Nelson-Hall.
Cho, Y. (2011). Desperately seeking east Asia amidst the popularity of South Korean pop culture in Asia. *Cultural Studies*, *25*(3), 383–404.
Day, T. (2002). *A century of recorded music: Listening to musical history*. New Haven, CT: Yale University Press.
Gaisberg, F. W. (1942). *The music goes round*. New York: Macmillan.
Gronow, P. (1981). The recording industry comes to the orient. *Ethnomusicology*, *25*(2), 251–284.
Han'guk pangsong simŭi wiwŏnhoe. (1981). *Pangsong kŭmji kayo mongnok illam*. Seoul: Han'guk pangsong simŭi wiwŏnhoe.
Harker, D. (1980). *One for the money: Politics and popular song*. London: Hutchinson.
Hesmondhalgh, D. (2013). *The cultural industries*. London: Sage.
Hong, E. (2014). *The birth of Korean cool*. New York: Picador.
Hübinette, T. (2012). The reception and consumption of hallyu in Sweden: Preliminary findings and reflections. *Korea Observer*, *43*(3), 503–525.
Hwang, M. (1989). *Han'guk taejung yŏnyesa*. Seoul: Puruganmoro.
Hwang, O. (2006). The ascent and politicization of pop music in Korea: From the 1960s to the 1980s. In K. Howard (Ed.), *Korean Pop Music: Riding the Wave* (pp. 34–47). Folkestone: Global Oriental.
Iwabuchi, K. (2002). *Recentering globalization: Popular culture and Japanese transnationalism*. Durham, NC: Duke University Press.
Jung, E.-Y. (2006). Articulating Korean youth culture through global popular music styles: Seo Taiji's use of rap and metal. In K. Howard (Ed.), *Korean pop music: Riding the wave* (pp. 109–122). Folkestone: Global Oriental.
Jung, S. (2011). *Korean masculinities and transcultural consumption: Yonsama, rain, oldboy and k-pop idols*. Hong Kong: Hong Kong University Press.
Jung, S., & Hirata, Y. (2012). Conflicting desires: K-pop idol flows in Japan in the Era of web 2.0'. *Electronic Journal of Contemporary Japanese Studies*, *12*(2). http://japanesestudies.org.uk/ejcjs/vol12/iss2/jung.html.
Kang, C. (1999). *Uri somanghaetta, noraehal chayurŭl, Chungang Ilbo, 27 August*.
Khiun, L. K. (2013). K-pop dance trackers and cover dancers: Global cosmopolitanization and local spatialization. In Y. Kim (Ed.), *The Korean wave: Korean media go global* (pp. 165–181). New York: Routledge.
Kim, C. 2000a. *Han'guk kayo chŏngsinsa*. Seoul: Arŭm ch'ulp'ansa.
Kim, C. (Ed.), (2000b). *Yusŏnggi ŭmban ch'ongnam charyojip*. Seoul: Sinnara.
Kim, H. (2001). *Sŏ T'aeji tamnon*. Seoul: Ch'aegi innŭn maŭl.
Kwon, H. (2014). *Cultural globalization and the Korean promotion policy for music based on tradition: A study of the activation plan and its background* (PhD dissertation). London: SOAS University of London.
Lee, K.-h. (2007). Looking back at the cultural politics of youth culture in South Korea in the 1990s: On the "new generation" phenomenon and the emergence of cultural studies. *Korean Journal of Communication Studies*, *15*(4), 47–79.
Lee, S. H. (2012). *The (geo)politics of beauty: Race, transnationalism and neoliberalism in South Korean beauty culture* (PhD dissertation). Ann Arbor, MI: University of Michigan.
Lie, J. (1992). The concept of mode of exchange. *American Sociological Review*, *57*(4), 508–523.

Maliangkay, R. (2006a). Supporting our boys: American military entertainment and Korean pop music in the 1950s and early 1960s. In K. Howard (Ed.), *Korean pop music: Riding the wave* (pp. 21–33). Folkestone: Global Oriental.
Maliangkay, R. (2006b). Pop for progress: Censorship and South Korea's propaganda songs. In K. Howard (Ed.), *Korean pop music: Riding the wave* (pp. 48–61). Folkestone: Global Oriental.
Maliangkay, R. (2014). The popularity of individualism: The Seo Taiji phenomenon in the 1990s. In K. Kim Hyun & Y. Choe (Eds.), *The Korean popular culture reader* (pp. 296–313). New York: Routledge.
Manuel, P. (1988). *Popular musics of the non-western world*. New York: Oxford University Press.
No, T. (1995). *Han'guk kŭndae ŭmaksa 1*. Seoul: Han'gilsa.
Oh, I., & Park, G.-S. (2012). From B2C to B2B: Selling Korean pop music in the age of new social media. *Korea Observer*, *43*(3), 365–397.
Pae, Y. (2011). *Han'guk yusŏnggi ŭmban*. Seoul: Han'gŏrŭm.1904–1945.
Pak, G. L. (2006). On the mimetic faculty: A critical study of the 1984 ppongtchak debate and post-colonial mimesis. In K. Howard (Ed.), *Korean pop music: Riding the wave* (pp. 62–71). Folkestone: Global Oriental.
Pak, C. (2009). *Han'guk kayosa 1894–1945, 1*. Seoul: Miji.
Pease, R. (2006). Internet Fandom and K-Wave in China. In K. Howard (Ed.), *Korean pop music: riding the wave* (pp. 176–189). Folkestone: Global Oriental.
Shin, H. (2009). Have you ever seen the rain? and who'll stop the rain? the globalizing project of Korean pop (K-pop). *Inter-Asia Cultural Studies*, *10*(4), 507–523.
Shin, H., & Kim, P. H. (2014). Birth, death, and resurrection of group sound rock. In K. Kim Hyun & Y. Choe (Eds.), *The Korean popular culture reader* (pp. 275–295). New York: Routledge.
Son, M.-J. (2006). Highway songs in South Korea. In K. Howard (Ed.), *Korean pop music: Riding the wave* (pp. 72–81). Folkestone: Global Oriental.
Tomlinson, J. (2003). Globalization and cultural identity. In D. Held & A. McGrew (Eds.), *The global transformations reader* (pp. 269–277). Cambridge: Polity Press.
Yamauchi, F. 2009a. *Ilchesigi han'guk nogŭm munhwa ŭi yŏksa minjokchi: Cheguk chilso wa misijŏngch'i*. Sŏngnam: Han'gukhak Chungang Yŏn'guwŏn. (PhD dissertation).
Yamauchi, F. 2009b. Ilchesigi ŭmban sanŏpkye-esŏ han'gugin chunggaeja ŭi yŏksajŏk chuch'esŏng koch'al. *Taejung ŭmak*, *4*, 97–184.
Yamauchi, F. (2011). Policing the sounds of colony: Documentary power and the censorship of korean recordings in the age of performative reproduction. *Musica humana*, 3.1, (pp. 83–120). Spring.
Yamauchi, F. (2012). (Dis)Connecting the empire: Colonial modernity, recording culture, and Japan-Korea musical relations. In H. de Ferranti & Y. Fumitaka (Eds.), *Colonial modernity and East Asian musics* (pp. 143–206). Berlin: Verlag für Wissenschaft und Bildung.
Yi, U. (1996). *PD Yi Uyong ŭi uri taejung ŭmak ilki*. Seoul: Ch'anggongsa.
Yi, Y. (1984). Ilche sidae ŭi taejung kayo. In K. Ch'angnam, et al. (Eds.), *Norae 1* (pp. 83–119). Seoul: Silch'ŏn munhaksa.
Yi, Y. (2000). *Han'guk taejung kayosa*. Seoul: Sigongsa.
Yi, Y. (2004). Norae insaeng 45-nyŏn, yŏngwŏnhan "Tongbaek agassi" Yi Mija. *Haep'i t'ugedŏ*, 22–55.

CHAPTER 7

Business Ethics and Government Intervention in the Market in *Joseon*

S. Kang*, J. Choi[†]
*Korea University, Seoul, South Korea
[†]Academy of Korean Studies, Seoul, South Korea

7.1 INTRODUCTION

Although large-scale East Asian wars plagued the Korean peninsula from the 16th century to early-17th century, the *Joseon* dynasty remained relatively unchanged during the 300 years since its founding in 1392. In the aftermath of these battles, the Ming dynasty collapsed as Qing seized control over the Central Plain [*Zhongyuan*] in China, while the Tokugawa Shogunate emerged from the ashes of the Toyotomi regime in Japan. What allowed *Joseon*, the smallest and most damaged of the three East Asian states, to continue to exist?

Some argued that this was made possible by a compromise, whereby elites accepted the legitimacy of the king and dynasty alongside compliance with a Sino-oriented tribute system in exchange for the preservation of existing privileges,[1] while others stressed the importance of mutual checks and balances between the king and bureaucrats.[2] Still others argued that it was *Joseon*'s economic base which contributed to the dynasty's longevity. Specifically, the king rented out land and public financial resources to the elite in exchange for their support, and also provided the people with public goods, such as the grain loan system [*hwangok*], to secure quasi-voluntary compliance.[3]

The views embedded in these studies represent a meaningful departure from existing mainstream studies, the latter of which employ an internal development theory that perceived late *Joseon* society as being marked by

[1]Palais (1999).
[2]Park (2004a, 2004b).
[3]Kim (2011).

the decline of feudalism and expansion of capitalism[4]. Internal development theory has underestimated late *Joseon*'s political and economic capabilities by viewing this period as one characterized by a lax ruling structure. Specifically, it has overlooked the fact that increased agricultural productivity and the development of a commodity-based economy were induced by strong fiscal policy, contrary to the notion of a weakening state.

Recent studies describing late *Joseon*'s economic structure as a national redistribution economy have also faced limitations. These studies have maintained that *Joseon* moved towards a redistribution economy that placed great importance on agriculture while cautioning against the pursuit of profit in accordance with its Confucian physiocracy. Furthermore, they have argued that there existed a national redistribution system characterized by a government procurement market in Seoul. This was rooted in fiscal payments and the provision of livelihood funds to peasant farmers by setting aside grain loans in local areas during late *Joseon*, when the market and finance were still in a nascent state.[5] The belief that *Joseon* represented a redistribution economy characterized by strong state intervention in the market is based on Polanyi,[6] with premodern economic integration based on the market, redistribution, and reciprocity, as well as peasant society theory, which has placed East Asian economic structures within an intensive agricultural management system framework.[7]

On the one hand, these studies have refuted the linear and European-centric development model that views the transition towards capitalism as an essential stage of historical development. Instead, they have focused on the uniqueness of Confucian states in East Asia, such as market intervention based on Confucian physiocracy. But although these studies have accepted the coexistence of the market and redistribution during late *Joseon*, they have been unable to explain this phenomenon. While the market and redistribution have been perceived as representing dominant and subsidiary elements, respectively, this chapter argues that the market and redistribution in late *Joseon* should be understood as interdependent elements, rather than reflecting a dominance-based relationship.

The *Daedongbeop* [Uniform Land Tax Law] was a reform of the tribute tax system designed to make the public pay taxes to the central government in grain, cloth, and coins instead of in local products. In addition,

---

[4]Kim(1970), Kang(1984).
[5]Lee (1996), Kim (2005), Lee and Park (2007), Lee (2010a, 2010b, 2012).
[6]Polanyi (1957).
[7]Miyajima (2009).

Seonhyecheong [Agency to Bestow Blessings] was the largest financial establishment in terms of the purchase and delivery of items needed by the royal family and government offices via the market in Seoul. For these reasons, the *Daedongbeop* and *Seonhyecheong* can be regarded as useful windows through which to analyze the relationship between national redistribution and the market in late *Joseon* as well as state management ethics.

To date, many studies have analyzed the goals, principles, and effects of the *Daedongbeop*.[8] Furthermore, others have examined revenue and expenditure structure, relations with other financial establishments, and management methods employed by *Seonhyecheong* in light of government procurement, market stimulus, and the stabilization of public livelihood.[9] However, there have been few studies that have undertaken analysis from the viewpoint of state managerial ethics.

Given the recent increase in studies focusing on the fiscal policy of late *Joseon* from the standpoint of relief policy and publicness,[10] this chapter presents a case study of the *Daedongbeop* and *Seonhyecheong* that analyzes management ethics adopted by the kings and elite of late *Joseon* and how they intervened in the market. This chapter undertakes archival research with a focus on analyzing the goals, impact, and management of the *Daedongbeop* and *Seonhyecheong*. Sources include government-led publications such as *Joseon Wangjo Sillok* [Annals of the *Joseon* Dynasty], *Seungjeongwon Ilgi* [Daily Records of the Office of Royal Secretariat], and *Jeungbo Munheon Bigo* [Revised and Enlarged Edition of the Reference Compilation of Documents on Korea].

In addition, this study frames the discussion within modes of exchange and moral persuasion developed by Lie.[11] Lie stressed that exchange could be regulated depending on social relations and the state's authority structure, and that each mode of exchange had its own moral persuasion. The multilayered coexistence of these modes of exchange can be used to explain the complex modes of late *Joseon*, which saw the state intervene in the market to restrain competition and support merchants. As such, this study should help explain how managerial ethics of *Joseon*'s ruling class, which sought to cling to the ideology of Confucian goodwill and use the market accordingly, contributed to the dynasty's longevity.

---

[8] Han (1978), Tokunari (1987), Lee (2010b).
[9] Park (2008), Park (2004a, 2004b), Choi (2014).
[10] Lee (2011), Song (2013).
[11] Lie (1992).

7.2 THE PRINCIPLE OF *DAEDONGBEOP* AND MANAGEMENT OF *SEONHYECHEONG* IN LATE *JOSEON*

7.2.1 Unpacking the Daedongbeop and Seonhyecheong

The enforcement of the *Daedongbeop* dramatically changed a tax collection system and ideology based on grain, corvée labor, and tributes [*joyongjo*] by transforming the local product in-kind system (which accounted for the largest portion of overall finance in-kind) into a land tax system. While the burden borne by the poor fell sharply, that of landowners increased as a result of its implementation. This may be the primary reason why it took around 100 years to extend the *Daedongbeop* nationwide after first being implemented in the *Gyeonggi* area in 1608.[12]

Prior to the *Daedongbeop*'s implementation, the practice of levying tributes from the people and mobilizing corvée labor in counties and prefectures included clauses that made it possible for farmers to prepare tributes and corvée labor for each 8-*gyeol* unit of land. To this end, the government identified heads of households responsible for collecting tributes and mobilizing corvée labor from individual land lots of 8-*gyeol*.[13] But despite the practice of sharing tax burdens, costs associated with the purchase and transport of goods remained high and were generally passed on to the poor. The burden on farmers grew further with the introduction of the exorbitant proxy tax [*bangnap*], which served as a substitute for goods deemed difficult to purchase. Furthermore, the central government continued to adhere to the practice of leaving unnecessary items on tributary ledgers, collecting them continuously, and even unnecessarily adding additional amounts.[14]

In light of this, the *Daedongbeop* was introduced to mitigate the abuses of the tributary system and to realize taxation equality by uniformly levying 12-*du* of rice for 1-*gyeol* of land in place of spot goods. But as this led to taxation being overly focused on land, local elites who possessed large amounts of land and those who had profited from the proxy tax payment system were most opposed to the *Daedongbeop*'s expansion. This is reflected in the appeal submitted by Jo Ik, a leading proponent of the reform's expansion, during the reign of King *Injo*:

> Those who are involved with the proxy tax payment, corrupt officials, and local powers will inevitably dislike this law [Daedongbeop]. However, the common people with no power will clearly welcome it... If these corrupt officials and local powers

---

[12]Han (1978).
[13]Lee (1980).
[14]Go (1985).

are allowed to let their greed run rampant to the point where these common people lose their livelihood, then we will indeed be living in troubled times. However, a world in which the common people can earn a living by not being subject to the rampant greed of these corrupt officials and local powers could only be defined as a peaceful one. The reason why I am pushing so hard for the enforcement of this law is that I desire to create a peaceful world through good governance. (Jo Ik, <Pojeojip [Collection of Jo Ik's works]>, Vol. 14, Nondaedong gyesa)

Thus following the footsteps of I *Wonik*, who had first implemented the *Gyeonggi Seonhyebeop* during the reign of *Gwanghaegun*, Jo Ik argued for further expansion of the *Daedongbeop*'s application during the reign of King *Injo*.[15] This was in light of the greed of elites and the benefits that commoners could achieve given the *Daedongbeop*'s objectives.

But as the *Daedongbeop* had effectively altered the foundation of the existing taxation system and fiscal policy rooted in finance in-kind, arguments began to surface regarding its implementation.[16] These include the debate that took place regarding the reform's implementation in the *Hoseo* area:

Although the tributary system was amended in 1623 when the tributary ledger became even more disorderly following the Hideyoshi Invasions, the inequality of the system only led to more disdain for it on the part of the people. In this regard, the majority of the participants who engaged in prolonged discussions on this issue agreed that the system should be promptly improved. Some of them said, 'The tributary ledger should be amended in accordance with the tradition of the late king, and the local products collected based on the amended version'. Others stated, 'It is difficult to suddenly amend the tributary ledger. As such, let us calculate the prices of tribute items over the period of a year so as to allocate them equally and then collect them as rice and cloth that would then be transported to Seoul. If the tribute items are purchased in the form of collected rice and cloth, this will eliminate abuses and embezzlement midway'. Various opinions were introduced and no conclusions were reached. Chief State Councilor Kim Yuk strongly pushed for the implementation of the Daedongbeop: 'Chungcheong Province's tributary system is even more disorderly. Let us implement the law in this province first as a trial'. The King asked many officials for their opinions on various occasions. Some of them said it would be convenient, while others stated that it would be inconvenient. The King finally made the decision to apply the Daedongbeop in the Hoseo region first after discussions with Kim Yuk and others on whether the law was convenient. (<Hyojong sillok [Annals of King Hyojong]>, Vol. 7, August 24, 2nd year of King Hyojong)

At the time, two proposals were introduced during discussions on the implementation of the *Hoseo Daedongbeop*. While both proposals were rooted in the understanding that the existing tributary system was plagued

---
[15] Lee (2010a).
[16] Kim (1971).

by abuse and caused discontent among the people, resulting opinions were divergent. One called for maintaining the basic framework of the tributary system while amending the tributary ledger to better reflect reality, while the other involved full-fledged implementation of the *Daedongbeop*.

Eventually, the *Daedongbeop* was implemented in the *Hoseo* area, as had been argued for by Kim Yuk and others, and those who had initially opposed its implementation recognized the reform's convenience and agreed to its extension to the *Jeolla* and *Gyeongsang* regions.[17] As a result, the *Daedongbeop* was extended to the *Gangwon, Chungcheong, Jeolla, Gyeongsang*, and *Hwanghae* areas in 1708 (34th year of King *Sukjong*) after having been introduced in the *Gyeonggi* area in 1608.

Fig. 7.1 illustrates the structure and principles behind the *Daedongbeop*. As shown in the figure, the *Daedongbeop* was designed to mitigate various abuses that emerged during the collection of tributes. These included the concentration of taxation in-kind on poor people, the heavy burden imposed on proxy tax payers, and corrupt practices by the central government of rejecting tributes for no specific reason and requiring additional tributes

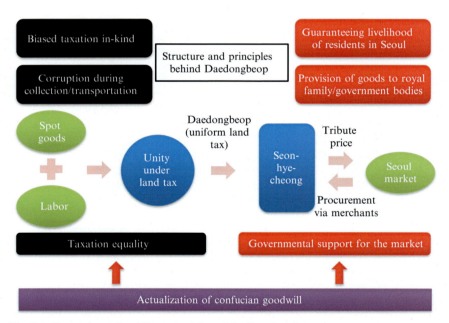

Fig. 7.1 Structure and guiding principles of the Daedongbeop.

[17]Lee (2010b).

when deemed necessary. In other words, the *Daedongbeop* was designed to bring about uniformity via taxation equality.

We can also uncover another aspect of the *Daedongbeop* by analyzing how financial resources collected in the name of the Uniform Land Tax [*Daedongse*] were actually spent. In late *Joseon*, the state established *Seonhyecheong* to manage financial resources collected through the *Daedongbeop*. The *Daedongbeop*'s implementation at the national level led to the prominence of *Seonhyecheong*, the latter of which grew to become the largest financial establishment by the early 18th century. In accordance with the Uniform Land Tax, it purchased and delivered necessities required by the royal family and governmental organizations from markets in Seoul. It designated merchants who would procure items included in the tributary ledger and paid these merchants four to five times higher than market prices.

The higher prices paid for tribute items reflected the government's intentions of guaranteeing the livelihood of residents in Seoul. As residents in Seoul did not farm land like those in local areas, they depended on being paid by the state for the cost of their labor. Merchants were also mobilized to engage in various kinds of corvée labor at the behest of the state. In exchange for this labor, they were allowed to participate in government procurement, receiving high wages for their services. In this sense, the market in Seoul was not mature enough to cover losses stemming from the government procurement process via private market exchange. As such, the *Joseon* government was required to support the market by paying higher prices.

Aside from *Seonhyecheong*'s primary purpose, the institution was also designed to respond to various demands of the state, including defense, diplomacy, and relief work. As its name implied, *Seonhyecheong* was in charge of distributing relief grain to the poor who poured into Seoul to flee from natural disasters and poor harvests, and employing laborers and paying them wages at the state's request. The *Joseon* government had previously established the *Jinhyeolcheong* [Relief Agency] as a temporary office to distribute grain in years of poor harvest, but this was passed on to *Seonhyecheong* after its establishment and integration with the *Jinhyeolcheong* in 1648.[18]

As such, the *Daedongbeop* was a measure that sought to decrease the burden of farmers by pursuing taxation equality and convenience, while also helping merchants and residents in Seoul sustain their livelihood. Thus, the *Daedongbeop* reflected the notion of Confucian goodwill under which benefits would be equally distributed among all people. Rather than representing

---

[18]Moon (1997).

an application to an already developed market for government procurement or to secure taxes once state intervention in the market had been abandoned, this was a taxation system designed to support agriculture in local areas and commerce in Seoul. Specifically:

> The Daedongbeop intended to correct the problems associated with the payment of taxes with goods… Rural peasants have now regained their will to survive, urban dwellers are becoming affluent, local rulers have become ethical again, demand and supply are in perfect harmony, merchants can barter freely, and people can rent out carts and ships to move their freight. All this means the whole economy is fair both from a horizontal and vertical standpoint. (Hong Bonghan, <Ikjeonggong jugo>)

Funds collected via the Uniform Land Tax were used to purchase tribute items as reserve grain during emergencies, and would serve as a reserve fund to cover financial shortages of other governmental departments. In addition, officials such as Hong praised the *Daedongbeop* as an institution that provided benefits to all people, including local residents, urban residents, magistrates, and merchants. *Seonhyecheong*, which was in charge of collecting the Uniform Land Tax, also played an important role in bringing about fairness from both a horizontal and vertical standpoint.

7.2.2 The Daedongbeop, Seonhyecheong, and Market Dynamism

As a result of the *Daedongbeop*'s implementation, we saw the emergence of a dynamic market in Seoul due to financial resources spent by government organizations, such as *Seonhyecheong* and the Ministry of Taxation. Commerce in Seoul's chartered market developed to the point where it was able to deliver various items needed by the royal family and government organizations. Private commerce also developed from the mid-17th century onwards, focusing on the delivery of daily necessities and items favored by residents in Seoul.

After the unofficial free market led by individual merchants began to develop from the late-17th century, we also saw the emergence of conflicts between government-licensed merchants and individual merchants.[19] In response, the government initially adopted a policy of protecting the chartered market by granting privileged positions to government-licensed merchants. However, it was becoming clear that individual merchants as well as merchants from the chartered market should be taken care of by the government. From the mid-18th century onwards, the government adopted a policy of

---

[19] Go (2013).

allowing freer trade by abolishing the privileges of participants in the chartered market, with the exception of the Six Licensed Stores [*Yukuijeon*].

In this sense, the *Daedongbeop* was not a measure applied to a developed market, but an effort to facilitate market development. A more dynamic market was made possible by the government's investment and support for the market, and not by policies designed to allow and facilitate free market competition. Thus, the market during late *Joseon* was marked by the intervention and management of its biggest purchaser, the government. Viewed from this standpoint, we can conclude that the ruling class of late *Joseon* accepted the ideology behind the manorial mode of exchange and recognized that the Confucian physiocracy that had prevailed at the beginning of the dynasty could no longer be realized. While market suppression created difficulties for farmers who served as direct producers, it also created the potential for corruption by the privileged few who served as intermediates between the state and producers.

During late *Joseon*, the market began to be perceived as a useful and effective system in terms of the exchange of goods. Here, the market was regarded as a space in which merchants who had to engage in corvée services for the state could establish supply-demand relations, and not a space for free competition between individual merchants freed from the limitations of social status. The privileged government-licensed merchants were not the only ones to receive help from state investment and support for the market; individual merchants also benefited from this arrangement.

Within the framework of modes of exchange, the mode in which the state strongly intervenes in the market and trades with merchants endowed with privileges can be regarded as the mercantile mode. At the same time, the government of late *Joseon* still pursued the manorial moral persuasion characterized by horizontal and vertical fairness instead of the mercantile moral persuasion marked by a wealthy state. This ideology and policy toward the market contributed to the longevity of the *Joseon* dynasty, but delayed the development of a merchant class that could expand capital, unfettered by government control.

7.3 STATE MANAGERIAL ETHICS AND MARKET PERCEPTIONS AS REFLECTED IN THE *DAEDONGBEOP*

From the outset, the *Joseon* government intended to establish a finance in-kind system in which the items required by the royal family and government were directly secured through the collection of tribute items.

In addition, the government established a policy of strong market intervention and control that was designed to maintain the social status of merchants while prohibiting the pursuit of excessive profits through abuse of market exchange.

On the other hand, it established privileged markets known as *sijeon* that were responsible for delivering specific goods not covered by tributes from local farmers. The government also purchased goods through the chartered market on specific occasions, such as the reception of foreign envoys or implementation of royal rites. But the government's procurement method faced growing criticism during the 16th century:

> I have heard that the merchants suffer as a result of the government's trade orders. Those who have stockpiled the necessary goods demand higher prices whenever the government submits a trade order. As a result, the price of such goods suddenly skyrockets four to five times higher... Those who are involved with the proxy tax payment [bangnap] hide the goods from the people in their houses. They request that merchants desiring to purchase these goods pay a much higher price than usual when the government submits a trade order. Then, after obtaining great profits from delivering these goods to the government, they wait until the prices go down again. These practices have led to great losses for the merchants, who are now afraid of the government's trade orders. Such social ills are similar to those found in the palace and capital markets [gongsi] of the Tang dynasty. Your highness does not know that this evil practice has been carried out in Seoul. How can you even begin to fathom the anger of soldiers and people in local areas? (Seong Hon, <Ugyejip [Collection of Seong Hon's Works]>, Vol. 3)

The term "trade" as understood in *Seong Hon's* petition did not refer to the exchange of goods and currency between individuals based on the principle of equality. The government's order to trade was in fact a request that government-licensed merchants within the chartered market deliver specific goods to the government at a cost.

Then why were government-licensed merchants afraid of receiving trade orders? While the government intended to pay for the goods at prevailing market prices, the merchants first had to purchase the desired items before they could sell them to the government. Whenever a trade order was submitted, individuals involved with the proxy tax payment system who possessed the necessary items demanded prices that were several times higher than market value. The government-licensed merchants from the chartered market [*sijeon sangin*] who depended on government procurement services inevitably incurred losses when procuring items needed by the government.

The market in Seoul had not yet developed when *Seong Hon* submitted this petition during the 16th century. As a result, the government-licensed merchants within the chartered market had to depend on proxy tax payers to conduct trade demanded by the government. These proxy tax payers colluded with the royal family or powerful families and stocked up goods in their houses while waiting for the government to submit trade orders. This would allow them to supply necessities to government-licensed merchants from the chartered market at higher prices. Furthermore, they also received payment after delivering goods to the government on behalf of people in local areas. Those who were involved with the proxy tax payment reaped profits from both sides (the government-licensed merchants from the chartered market and the people in local areas) during the period marked by governmental control of the market and management of finance in-kind.

Thus, the *Daedongbeop* served as a tool to curtail covert practices, like the proxy tax payment [*bangnap*] system, by officially purchasing necessities from the market at prices four to five times in excess. But perhaps the more important effect of the *Daedongbeop* was to shift perceptions of the market and commerce in a more positive light. *Yu Hyeongwon* postulated that the implementation of the *Daedongbeop* would stimulate the market and the flow of goods and currency:

> *Someone says, 'The distribution of goods is not as well carried out in Korea as in China. In this regard, no matter how much is paid out, goods will not make their way to Seoul and there are worries that the government organization will not receive necessities in time if all kinds of goods are purchased solely from the market in Seoul.' This sounds plausible. Such a situation might have emerged when this law (Daedongbeop) was first implemented. However, such rumors will no longer be heard in two to three years and local products will flow to the market. The failure to secure goods in the past can be traced back to the purchase of goods at proper prices. Because of its geographical features, Korea has a patchy road system and, therefore, its transportation network is less developed than China's. However, people the world over possess the same mindset in that they pursue profit while eschewing losses. Therefore, if the prices are high enough, people will naturally gather in places where they can pursue such profits. There is no way of stopping them. As such, someone's saying is not quite right. Currently, the goods in kind from local areas account for not even 1-2% of the goods collected from the government's tributary system. The majority of these goods were purchased in Seoul and provided by proxy tax payers who received bribes. I am sure that this practice will disappear [when the Daedongbeop is implemented and extended]. (Yu Hyeongwon, <Bangye Surok [Yu Hyeongwon's Treatises]>)*

The *Daedongbeop*'s implementation and subsequent high payment for goods ensured that goods naturally made their way to Seoul even though

the government no longer forced through any such trade. In other words, the government could purchase necessities in the market in Seoul. Those such as *Yu Hyeongwon* did not view merchants' commercial activities and pursuit of profits negatively. Rather, the stimulation of the market by using such motives would enable the state to provide necessities through the market and also prevent corruption among proxy tax payers.

Seoul's market size increased alongside its rising population, and the *Daedongbeop*'s implementation was accompanied by the establishment of military and administrative bodies inside and outside the capital fortress. Rice, cloth, and coins collected nationwide as a result of the *Daedongbeop* were amassed in storage facilities of *Seonhyecheong*. *Seonhyecheong* prepaid the tribute merchants [*gongin*] and government-licensed merchants from the chartered market for their procurement services, with prices reflecting the price of actual tributes and service costs.

But although the *Daedongbeop* was designed to deliver necessities to the government in a stable manner and maintain living standards of merchants by supporting the market, many problems emerged. The biggest problem was that while procurement pricing for necessities paid out by *Seonhyecheong* remained the same as when the *Daedongbeop* was first implemented, prices of goods distributed in the market rose over time. Market prices for goods which *Seonhyecheong* purchased via prepayment also rose. Market participants knew that the government's procurement pricing was higher than market prices, and prices of agricultural products skyrocketed in years marked by poor harvest.

This resulted in an extra burden on tribute merchants responsible for delivering tribute items. While the costs that tribute merchants had to incur for the procurement of such items increased, procurement pricing set by *Seonhyecheong* remained unchanged. As such, from the early 18th century onwards, there was a marked increase in the number of merchants who fled because they could not deliver tribute items even after being prepaid by *Seonhyecheong*.

Rather than raising the prices of tribute items, the government sought to rectify this situation by improving the trade environment. This included the eradication of miscellaneous tasks imposed on tribute merchants and the prohibition of government officials' covert demands for goods. The government could not raise prices of procurement tributes because it had to apply austerity measures to avoid increasing the burden on local farmers.

Seeking to stabilize prices, the government officially recognized merchants' right to pursue profits in the market to some extent and allowed

them to freely distribute goods in the late 18th century. The most representative of these measures was the implementation of commercial equalization. This policy partially abolished the privilege of unofficial private markets given to government-licensed merchants in the chartered market,[20] and created an opportunity for residents in Seoul to participate in commercial activities. This policy was also pursued by King Jeongjo at the end of the 18th century, and by 1791, the government announced the *Sinhae Tonggong*, effectively curbing all privileges given to government-licensed merchants, with the exception of the Six Licensed Stores [*Yukuijeon*].

The government of late *Joseon* changed existing market policies to respond to the growing number of merchants taking part in government procurement services, as well as those in Seoul who earned a living from the naturally-formed markets along the Han River and around the capital fortress. During discussions on measures that should be prepared with regard to grain needed by residents of Seoul, King Jeongjo issued a royal decree in 1791:

> *The price of grain should remain low enough to ensure that the residents of Seoul do not starve. However, three potential pitfalls exist, namely tribute merchants [gongin], the market, and merchants. In accordance with a recent report by the Censorate, I have ordered the relevant administrative officials to stop raising the prices of grain. However, this will in all likelihood not have the desired effects… If a prohibitive law against the pursuit of profits is enacted, then merchants engaged in transporting the goods to Seoul by boats and carts will simply give up and go back to commerce. The government's storage of all the necessary grain is also an errant strategy. It is essential that we get merchants to voluntarily move to Seoul. This will be akin to piling up millions of grain in the market. Once the price of grain is stabilized in the market, we will be able to ensure a steady supply to the entire nation…. I have heard that the people of Seoul have had a hard time making a living. That is why I am asking you [central officials] for methods to gather grain in Seoul. The government should be well aware of my intentions and apply them nationwide. Let the merchants hear these rumors and gather in Seoul so that we can provide grain to the people of Seoul. (Jeongjo Sillok [Annals of King Jeongjo], Vol. 32, August 24, 1792)*

King *Jeongjo* suggested measures to allow and encourage merchants in local areas to move to Seoul so that they could trade grain in the market. He believed that grain prices in Seoul would naturally fall if the government allowed free trade of grain. By the late 18th century, *Joseon* dynasty kings were aware that the market, rather than a place to be controlled, was a place

[20]Kim (2010).

where goods were naturally distributed by merchants engaging in commercial activities and pursuing profit.

Then why did the *Joseon* government change its policy from regulating the market to supporting and stimulating it? This was not because the state abandoned benevolent governance or Confucian goodwill, where the state was perceived as the main actor responsible for public livelihood and redistribution. Rather, the government deemed it necessary to realize the protection of public livelihood and state redistribution through the market:

> *The market is a place where people buy and sell goods and helps to supply necessities to the government. The grain loan system revolves around the state's loosening and tightening of the grain supply. The life and death of people are dependent on this… Our government has placed great importance on this. In this regard, the provision of relief to the people of Seoul had the effect of further solidifying the foundation of the state. Furthermore, the management of the grain loan system was regarded as being of great importance, with the proper management of the system leading to the establishment of necessary relations between the state and people. Trade along the border area became an important issue in foreign relations. The provision of relief from bad harvests is a benevolent political act designed to protect the people. As such, the ancestral kings never refrained from sincerely engaging in their responsibilities. Our king had a good understanding of these issues and corrected the wrongdoings, showing great flexibility in the process. (<Jeungbo Munheon Bigo [Revised and Enlarged Edition of the Reference Compilation of Documents on Korea]>, Vol. 163, Sijeokgo)*

Thus, by the late 18th century, the market was viewed as a place where people bought and sold goods, the government secured necessities, and the management of financial measures was facilitated. Separately, the grain loan system [*hwangok*] represented a relief measure designed to ensure the people's survival by releasing grain during the spring famine and then redeeming them in autumn. On one level, the market (where goods were exchanged for profits) and the grain loan system (through which the state actualized redistribution) can be seen as having employed different mechanisms. However, they were also seen as having shared common elements in that they contributed to state financial management and maintenance of public livelihood. This is one of the reasons that the *Jeungbo Munheon Bigo* combined the market and grain loan system [*hwangok*] as "*sijeok.*"[21]

Through this review, we have seen that the government of late *Joseon* changed its perceptions and policy toward the market. The commercial policy of early *Joseon*, which was designed to suppress and control merchants,

---

[21]Lee (1996).

entered a new phase as a result of the *Daedongbeop*'s implementation. In order to ensure a steady flow of necessities from procurement merchants, the government established prices that were higher than those found in the market. It also curtailed harmful practices of mobilizing merchants for various forms of corvée labor and tasking them with the collection of additional goods. By the late 18th century, market intervention had been modified based on the policy of *Tonggong*, under which the residents of Seoul could freely participate in market exchange and equally pursue profit. In addition, the government of late *Joseon* made efforts to effectuate the Confucian ideology of benevolent governance by making use of the seemingly conflicting market and grain loan systems [*hwangok*].

7.4 CONCLUSION

This study analyzed the management of the *Daedongbeop* and *Seonhyecheong* and their contribution to *Joseon*'s longevity in the face of large-scale, regional wars. It also examined state managerial ethics pursued by *Joseon* dynasty's ruling elites within the framework of modes of exchange.

Joseon's refusal to abandon the finance in-kind system and continuous intervention in the market was not rooted in actual or perceived effectiveness of such moves. Rather, these represented an integral part of state managerial ethics established by the ruling elites based on the notion of Confucian goodwill, under which the state and king are responsible for public livelihood and are active in the distribution of goods and resources. This ethic made it possible for *Joseon* to pursue greater market intervention vis-à-vis other East Asian countries through the defense of manorial and mercantilist modes of exchange.

Specifically, the *Joseon* dynasty implemented the *Daedongbeop* to mitigate difficulties and problems associated with the existing tributary system. The law brought about a shift in perceptions and policies governing the market and commerce. The government aimed to ensure a smooth supply of necessities required by the royal family and government through the market, and to make it possible for those in Seoul not engaged in farming to secure their livelihood through commercial activities and services. To achieve this, the government established prices for the procurement goods that were well above market value.

However, this also caused difficulties for some tribute merchants [*gongin*]. These merchants found that they could not generate profit because the government's fixed prices for procurement goods did not take inflation into

consideration. Rather than raising prices of procurement goods, the government prohibited and more closely monitored corrupt practices that impeded on the rights of tribute merchants. Furthermore, the government also released grain in poor harvest years to ensure public livelihood and sustenance. It rigidly cracked down on market disturbances, such as when a specific party intentionally raised market prices by purchasing a large amount of goods. Thus, state intervention in the market did not cease even after the implementation of the *Daedongbeop*.

The increase in the size and function of the government procurement market had the secondary effect of leading to the development of unofficial free markets in Seoul. This led to deepening conflicts between procurement merchants who were granted privileges from the government and small-scale merchants who participated in the free markets. But by the late 18th century, the government had implemented the *Tonggong* policy which curbed all privileges given to government-licensed merchants, with the exception of those belonging to the Six Licensed Stores. This move was designed to curb profit monopolization by certain merchants in order to share market profits with the majority of residents in Seoul.

The government of late *Joseon* also resolved new problems that emerged from the *Daedongbeop*'s implementation, all while maintaining the notion of horizontal and vertical farness. While these efforts led to the expansion of the market in Seoul, the government's intention to support the market was based on the desire for prompt distribution of goods and balanced redistribution, rather than a move towards market or entrepreneurial modes of exchange.

In this respect, longstanding adherence to this state managerial ethic by the kings and ruling elites of *Joseon* can be traced back to Confucian goodwill. Although there were kings and officials who did not abide by their moral responsibilities, *Joseon*'s state system never completely abandoned this ideology. As such, the Confucian ethical persuasion helped *Joseon* to hold on to firm manorial and mercantile rule in East Asia, even as China lifted its ban on the market economy, and maintained its hold going into the 19th century. For the purposes of this chapter, it can be argued that it was this ethic that contributed to allowing the *Joseon* dynasty to endure for some 500 years.

While the financial structure of late *Joseon* was able to maintain a balance between intervention in and support for the market, it encountered a crisis from the 19th century in the form of financial deficit. This was the result of continued adherence to a policy of supporting and controlling the market, a policy whose management costs increased over time. The stiffening of

state power from the 19th century onwards further intensified this dilemma amidst internal conflict, and we would see the *Joseon* dynasty effectively lose its moral authority and struggle to survive.

REFERENCES

Choi, J. (2014). *Joseonhugi Seonhyecheong-ui unyoung-gwa joungangjaejeong gujo-ui byeonhwa* [The implementation of Seonhyechung and the transformation of Late Joseon Dynasty's financial structure]. (Ph.D. dissertation). Seoul: Korea University.
Go, S. (1985). 16~17 segi Gongnapje gaehyuk-ui banghyang [A new direction for reformed tributary systems during the 16th to 17th centuries]. *Hankuksaron*, *12*, 173–230.
Go, D. (2013). *Joseonsidae sijeonsangeop-yeongu* [A study on licensed shop commerce in the Joseon Dynasty]. Seoul: Jisiksaneopsa.
Han, Y. (1978). Daedongbeop-ui silsi [The implementation of Daedong System]. *Hankuksa*, *13*, 146–215.
Kang, M. (1984). *Joseon sidae sanggongeopsa-yeongu* [A study on the history of commerce & handicrafts in Korea's Yi Dynasty]. Seoul: Hangilsa.
Kim, Y. (1970). *joseonhugi nongeopsahweisa yeongu* [Agrarian history of the Late Yi Dynasty]. Seoul: Iljogak.
Kim, Y. (1971). Daedongbeop sihang-eul dulreossan chanban yangron-gwa gue baegyeong [Reasons and background behind disputes on the Daedongbeop]. *Daedongmoonhwa-yeongu*, *8*, 131–161.
Kim, J. (2005). Jeontongjeok gyeongjechaeje-ui jeonhwan: Jaebunbaegyeongje-eseo sijanggyeongje-ro [Transformation of the traditional economic system: Redistribution to market]. In L. Daegeun (Ed.), *Saeroun Hangukgyeongjebaljeonsa*. [New history of Korean economic development]. Seoul: Nanam Press.
Kim, J. (2010). *Jeongjodae Tonggong jeongchaek-ui sihang-e gwanhan yeongu* [Research on the Tonggong Policy of the King Jeongjo in Chosen Dynasty]. (Ph.D. dissertation). Seoul: Kookmin University.
Kim, J. (2011). Joseonwangjo janggijisok-ui gyeongjejeok giwon [Economic origins of the longevity of Joseon Dynasty (1392~1910) in Korea]. *Gyeongjehak-yeongu*, *59*(4), 53–117.
Lee, Y. (1980). Joseonhugi palgyeoljakbuje-e gwanhan yeongu [A study on the Jakbu System of the late Yi Dynasty]. *Hankuksa-yeongu*, *29*, 75–137.
Lee, H. (1996). Joseonsidae kukga-ui jaebunbae ginueug-gwa kuknae sangeop jeongchaek [Redistributive function of the state and commercial politics in Joseon Period]. *Sunggok Nonchong*, *27*, 451–489.
Lee, H. (2010a). Joseonwangjo-ui gyeongjetonghabcheje-wa geu byeonhwa-e gwanhan yeongu [The system of economic integration and its change in the Chosen Dynasty]. In H. Lee (Ed.), *Joseonhugi jaejeong-gwa sijang – Gyeongjechejeron-ui jeopgeun*. [The relations between the Chosen Dynasty finance and its market]. Seoul: Seoul National University Press.
Lee, J. (2010b). Joseonsidae gongmulbyeontongnon-eseo Pojeo Jo-Ik-ui wichi-wa yeokhal [The position and role of Pocho Cho Ik for the reformism of the Tribute Tax System in Choson Period]. *Daedongmoonhwa-yeongu*, *70*, 255–286.
Lee, J. (2011). Daedongbeop-eul tonghaeso bon Joseonsidae gonggongseong gwannyeom-gwa hyeonsil [The idea and reality of the public represented through the Tadong Law]. *Yuksa Bipyeong*, *94*, 104–127.
Lee, J. (2012). *Daedongbeop: Joseon choego-ui gaehyeok – Baekseong-eun meogeul geuseul haneulro samneunda* [Daedongbeop: The best reform of Joseon]. Seoul: Yuksa Bipyeongsa.
Lee, Y., & Park, Y. (2007). 18 segi Joseonwangjo-ui gyeongjecheje: Gwangyeokjeok tonghapchegye-ui teukjil-eul jungsimeuro [Economic system of Choson Dynasty in the

18th century]. In S. Nakamura & S. Park (Eds.), *Geundae dongasia gyeongje-ui yeoksajeok gujo*. [Historical structure of Modern East Asian Economy]. Seoul: Iljogak.

Lie, J. (1992). The concept of mode of exchange. *American Sociological Review, 57*(4), 508–523.

Miyajima, H. (2009). Bunbae-wa jemin: Yugyo-ui jeminsasang-gwa sonongsahweron [Thought of relieving the people's suffering and peasant society theory in Confucianism]. *Gukhak-yeongu, 14*, 289–318.

Moon, Y. (1997). Joseonhugi sangjingok-ui seolchi [The establishment of Sangjingok in the Late Joseon Dynasty]. *Sachong, 46*, 113–145.

Palais, J. B. (1999). Joseonwangjo-ui gwallyojeok gunjuje [Bureaucratic monarchy of Joseon Dynasty]. In J. sidae sahakhwe (Ed.), *Dongyang samguk-ui wanggwon-gwa gwallyoje*. [Regal power and bureaucracy of three nations in East Asia]. Seoul: Gukhakjaryowon.

Park, G. (2008). Seonhyecheong-ui suip-gwa jichul [Revenue and expenditure of Seonhyechung]. *Seoulhak-yeongu, 32*, 73–109.

Park, H. (2004a). Joseonwangjo-ui janggijisokseong yoin yeonggu 1: Gongronjeongchi-reul jungsimeuro [Study on the background of the longevity in Joseon Dynasty: Focused on expostulation politics of Confucian intellectuals]. *Hankukhakbo, 30*(1), 31–61.

Park, S. (2004b). 17 segihuban hojo-ui jaejeongsuip hwakbochaek [The policy of Hojo to build up public finance in the Late 17th century Chosŏn Dynasty]. *Joseonsidaesahakbo, 31*, 113–141.

Polanyi, K. (1957). *The great transformation: The political and economic origins of our time*. Boston, MA: Beacon Press.

Song, Y. (2013). 18 segi Bichongje-ui jeokyoung-gwa jeminjeongchak-ui chujin [The application of the Bichong System and promotion of Jeminhwa Policy during the 18th century]. *Hankuksahakbo, 53*, 323–353.

Tokunari, T. (1987). Joseonhugi-ui Gongmul Munabje: gongin-yeongu-ui jeonjejakeopeuro [On the system of Gongmul Munap in the Late Joseon Dynasty: A prelude on the study of Gongin]. *Yeoksahakbo, 113*, 1–57.

CHAPTER 8

The Politics of Institutional Restructuring and Its Moral Persuasion in Japan: The Case of the Iron and Steel Industry (1919–34)

P. von Staden
KEDGE Business School, Marseille, France

8.1 INTRODUCTION

In his seminal work on "modes of exchange," Lie (1992) outlines how paradigmatic shifts in the structure of markets, opportunities for creating new networks, and the establishment of new modes of exchange are interrelated. Ultimately, the analysis of this dynamic serves to draw to the fore the underlying "social relations and social structures" and their change (Lie, 1992, p. 510). In the passage from one mode to the next, these transformations develop through a power struggle that takes place between stakeholders, two important ones being political authority and business (Lie, 1992, pp. 511–512). In this, limited attention is devoted to explaining the modalities of that struggle and, in turn, it is here that we propose to focus. In particular, we will address the role of the "moral imperative" and how this is exercised under conditions when government is not only responsible for the rationalization of the iron and steel industry, but also the dominant business stakeholder in that same industry.

As we will see through our case study on the amalgamation of Japan's iron and steel industry (1919–34), the role of the morally-based argument is an important explanatory factor in the shift from an entrepreneurial to a mercantile mode of exchange. Much of the struggle that transpired between government and business in this transition revolved around financial calculations. On this basis, as long as business reasoned that it made more sense

to ignore government demands, it did so. This independence was maintained despite a sustained decade-long government appeal to widely accept morally-based arguments.

The tide only shifted in the government's favor when two things happened, namely, that the private sector's calculation changed towards amalgamation and that the ideological basis of the moral imperative argument strengthened. These two factors underscore the central point of this chapter, which is that the persuasiveness of a morally-based argument is a function of its perceived validity in relation to its countervailing force(s). Like a seesaw, as one side strengthens, the other declines. By extension, seen from the government perspective, the associated politics becomes one of both, seeking ways to increase the persuasiveness of the moral reasoning and at the same time find ways to reduce impediments—financial or otherwise—that would give reason to business not to follow government wishes.

The mode of exchange springs from the characteristics of the market. Effectively, the exchange mode is an equilibrium point between ideas, structures, and actor interests. While it is beyond the scope or intent of this chapter to consider the "interests versus ideas" debate, our starting point is to observe that in negotiations, government uses ideas-based arguments that may lead to new modes of exchange, more from being that which we call the "moral imperative." It is an argument whose strength draws from its commonly agreed moral base and its pressing need for implementation. This is illustrated in the transition of Japan's market during the early years of its industrialization.

The market's raison d'être, or ideological underpinning, frames intra-market dynamics. As Lie points out, resource allocation is more complex than the neo-classical economics' depiction of autonomous rational actors seeking to maximize their utility. Transaction choices are value-laden and one critical component that informs these decisions is the ideological underpinning of the market. More concretely, the "moral imperative" argument may be exercised by government in a variety of circumstances, one being when national sovereignty is threatened. This may be when war looms or, in our case, the call for industrialization to strengthen a nation from within. At time of war, for example, the sequestering of private property for national interest may be sanctioned in law but, as is our case, the threat to national sovereignty is less direct albeit not necessarily less threatening. As we will see, the morally-based argument drew its strength from the need to achieve greater aggregate sector output through increased efficiency.

In the particular case of the restructuring of Japan's iron and steel industry, government negotiated from a moral high ground whose position stemmed from two factors. First, national aspirations of modernization expressed in slogans such as fukoku kyōhei (rich nation, strong army) and shokusan kōgyō (production promotion) had long-shaped Japan's domestic and foreign policies, one critical facet being industrialization (Samuels, 1994). The second was government-owned and -operated Yawata, the industry's largest integrated producer. Thus, government both operated with the mandate to realize national aspirations and, in terms of its demands for greater efficiency in the industry, stood on moral high ground as it was the largest integrated producer. When government called on business to "rationalize" its use of resources, the term "efficiency" took on greater weight. In the context of fukoku kyōhei, for example, these terms carried the force of the moral imperatives of sovereignty and modernity and, as recognized agents of national development, businessmen were called upon to fulfill their enlightened duties.

The moral imperative argument will be examined through the debates between government and business over the industry's amalgamation in the records of the shingikai, or Councils of Deliberation. In this legislatively-enshrined forum for extra-parliamentary consultation, attention will be paid to business and government debates over the protection and reorganization of the industry and how amalgamation was reached. The intent is that through the examination of these issues, we can understand how government and business arrived at a new mode of exchange in this industry.

8.2 ENTREPRENEURIAL MODE OF EXCHANGE: SURVIVAL BEFORE RATIONALIZATION (1919–25)

In the transition from one mode of exchange to the next, government and business are treated by Lie as separate entities each having its own sets of interests. While a political authority exercises regulatory and law making powers to frame how transactions take place within the market, business is focused on market transactions and pursuing its ends through political means. The lines of this delineation, however, are blurred in the case of the iron and steel industry. The prospects of both government and business zig-zagged between these categories drawing into question how interests were formed. Also, the entrepreneurial mode of exchange is characterized by a limited presence of government in market activity and that transactions typically take place between a small and stable number of actors at the local level.

Prior to the outbreak of World War I, these conditions were largely met. Given the industry's high market entry barrier, many entrepreneurs found startup costs too high. However, as we will see, the increased demand for iron and steel to meet the needs of Europe's war was sufficient to draw many new and small entrants into the industry. Spurred by short-term gains, concern for efficiency was a distant second worry for the young start-ups and the industry's producers increased dramatically during the war years. This influx exacerbated the industry's existing inefficiencies. In the context of the larger national aspirations of industrialization, the industry's structural imbalance and plethora of inefficient producers was deeply troubling for government. Although the logic of rationalization was clear, these arguments held little sway over producers whose prime concern was economic survival. Amalgamation of the industry as called for by government would have brought widespread suffering for the private sector.

With our focus on these two issues, we turn to the negotiating table. These issues came to the fore in the discussions of the Temporary Investigation Committee on Fiscal Policy and the Economy that ran from Sep. 1919 to Feb. 1921 (see Appendix 8.1). Membership of the Committee was finalized in September of 1919. There were 28 standing members, headed by Prime Minister Hara Kei as chairman and Takahashi Korekiyo, Minister of Finance, and Yamamoto Tatsuo, Minister of Agriculture and Commerce, as vice-chairmen. There were also 29 temporary members who were called up on an individual basis to participate in discussions if their presence was required. Secretaries were drawn from the Ministry of Agriculture and Commerce, Home Affairs, Ministry of Finance (Tax Bureau chief and Finance Bureau chief) and the cabinet secretary (refer to Appendix 8.2 for a large sample of the participant's backgrounds).

It is noteworthy that three of these members were at the time or would later in their careers become prime ministers. Seven participants had been, or would later, be cabinet ministers, and in several cases occupied ministerial posts a number of times. Similarly, if the categories of "financier," "businessmen," "banker," and "manager" were drawn together, we would see that at least eight had, or would hold, executive-level positions in major companies. In terms of balancing membership between the two sides of the bicameral system, we see rough parity in terms of numbers: Hara Kei, Hamaguchi Osachi, and Okazaki Kunisuke from the Lower House, and Takahashi Korekiyo, Yamamoto Tatsuo, Hashimoto Keizaburō, and Den Kenjirō from the Upper House, were representatives at the time of the deliberations.

The selection of committee membership suggests that importance was assigned to drawing together participants who were leading figures in their fields and to providing some balance between government and business representation in the broad sense. Thus there was a tendency for leading figures to have career paths that crisscrossed over the lines that delineated government and business. Beyond this, though, is the issue of what this blurred distinction means for our understanding of the moral imperative argument. As one form of the political struggle that drives the entrepreneurial mode of exchange on to the next, the deeper significance revolves around whether the political authority of government is so compromised to render Lie's distinction moot and, if so, how persuasive does the moral imperative argument become under these conditions?

For many of the private sector firms that had sprung up during the lucrative war years and now facing bankruptcy, there was a tendency to seek economic stability under the wing of the zaibatsu in order to gain financial support (Yonekura, 1994, pp. 93–96). By 1923, given the recession, "only nine iron producers, 22 crude steel producers, and 21 finished steel producers remained in the industry. Even larger firms, like Mitsubishi Steel and NKK [Japan Steel-Tube, Inc.], were forced to carry out a capital reduction" (Yonekura, 1994, pp. 86–88). Thus, this reorganization of the industry implied a diminution in the number of actors and, in turn, an increase in the concentration of influence in the hands of fewer firms.

In terms of the percentage of total domestic production, the war years also saw the relative strength between private sector and government shift away from Yawata. In 1913, Yawata's share of pig iron production was 73%, which diminished to 47% in 1919. Similarly, in 1913, Yawata's share of steel production was 85%, but by 1919 was 51% (Tsūshō Sangyōshō, 1970, p. 195). By 1926, despite the changes driven by domestic and international factors, economic and otherwise, Yawata still occupied a large position in the domestic market: (1) in terms of total domestic pig iron production, Yawata's share was 65.9%, while the aggregate production of the three principle private sector producers (Kamaishi, Wanishi, and Toyo) was 32.9%, with 1.2% held by others; (2) as for crude steel, Yawata held 62.5%, while the aggregate production of 10 principal private sector firms was 33.8% and 3.7% held by others; and (3) Yawata's share of finished steel production was 52.9%, while 11 other companies produced 40.5% and other minor firms were 6.6% (Yonekura, 1994, p. 97).

Though Yawata continued to be the single largest domestic producer in both iron and steel manufacture, in comparison to its prewar strength,

its position during the recession had been reduced. The aggregate production of all private sector manufacturers approached half of domestic output. Moreover, in terms of the number of actors, this gain in sway was focused in the hands of fewer firms. Thus, in terms of impact on the negotiation position of the private sector, though the firms were eager for government aid, they were not without strength (Yonekura, 1994, p. 85).

Despite the length of this shingikai, there was little time devoted to the issue of amalgamation. The foremost reason was that the dominant and immediate concern of both Yawata and the private sector was the agreement on tariff measures to protect the industry from international competition. That being said, as discussions turned to the details of the issue of amalgamation, talks became more specific. Members had before them a number of proposals and debate revolved around their relative merits. One concern was with Yawata's adaptability to demands driven by war. Imaizumi Kaichirō, Managing Director and Chief Engineer of NKK, stated that in his opinion, Yawata would be able to modify output to match demand shifts. He also raised a few points that deserved consideration: (1) if there are certain products that Yawata cannot produce, machines will be out of use and people unemployed. If it is inconvenient to transfer the resources to Yawata, this may have a significant impact and in this light amalgamation should be considered; (2) when would it be most convenient and optimal timing for companies to amalgamate, would not all be the same; and (3) according to proposal number two, it will secure the supply of resources which is a problem for Japanese sites, and this is an important first step in the amalgamation process (Rinji zaisei keizai chōsakai, 1919, pp. 55–56). At this juncture, then, we can see signs of division despite the reduced number of members from big business and that they had close and long-standing ties with government.

Notwithstanding the presence of leading politicians, some of whom were strong advocates of amalgamation, little success was seen. Towards the end of discussions, Imaizumi was asked about what he knew of government's opinion regarding amalgamation (Rinji zaisei keizai chōsakai, 1919, p. 55). Imaizumi replied that "it is a matter regarding the approval of the Minister of Finance, and also Shibusawa [Eiichi] will talk with Prime Minister Hara and the Minister of Finance" (Rinji zaisei keizai chōsakai, 1919, p. 55). Takahashi Korekiyo, a vice-chairman of this shingikai and the Finance Minister at that time, was a noted supporter of amalgamation. According to Okazaki, in each of the 1922 Eastern sea, China, and Osaka-Kyoto Seiyūkai party meetings, Takahashi as party president "stated the necessity for the amalgamation of the iron and steel industry" (Okazaki, 1984, p. 4).

Yet, despite the support of Imaizumi and the strongly-held position of Takahashi, amalgamation was not possible in the first half of the 1920s. Challenging "the common view that Mitsui and Mitsubishi supported the merger" of the iron and steel industry, Okazaki evaluates that because of the opposition of these two zaibatsu, amalgamation could not be realized. The financial position, he argues, of these large firms combined at that time was such that it was not necessary to enter into joint management with Yawata and other members of the industry (Okazaki, 1984, p. 17). The implication is that as long as the large zaibatsu had sufficient financial strength, despite whatever influence government may apply, they remained independent actors in the decision-making process, each with positions of influence stemming from either legislation or economic strength.

The politics of the proposed institutional restructuring of the iron and steel industry in the first half of the 1920s highlights the vulnerability of the actors operating under the conditions of the entrepreneurial mode of exchange. As Lie argues, in this mode, their numbers are small and stable. As the case of the iron and steel industry points out, these factors are closely related to the third factor of size, a proxy for financial strength. The inclination of business is to exercise the levers of political influence at its disposal to chart a course between receiving government aid of one form or another and, at the same time, retaining as much independence as possible. From the government perspective, the persuasiveness of the moral argument, even if its strength is drawn from the imperative of fukoku kyōhei is as effective as its ability to reduce the impact of the countervailing factors. Although the delineation between government and business is blurred in our case, for reasons of prospects and that government also is an industry stakeholder, those who have political authority also carry responsibility.

The political dynamics we have seen underscore that fulfilling that responsibility is a calculation between competing ends. Government is confronted with two moral choices: (1) provide economic succor and protection; and (2) rationalize the industry. Both are imperatives and at odds with each other; the first is immediate and the second more distant, albeit no less important. It is here, in the choice between the two, that we may speculate that the blurred delineation between government and business plays a role. One potential ancillary role that the forum of the shingikai provides for participants is that it avails them the opportunity to engage in face-to-face, off-the-record discussions. Here, personal connections (and obligations) that stem from their varied careers may too have played a part.

8.3 MERCANTILE MODE OF EXCHANGE: RATIONALIZATION GAINS SALIENCE (1926–34)

Lie explains that in the transition to the mercantile mode, there is an increased stratification of the market accompanied by a growing prominence of elites who establish close relationships with the central political authority. In our case study, we see the development of these characteristics emerge as the pressure of the continued economic downturn and the need to reorganize the industry eventually leads to its amalgamation realized through the shingikai forum (see Appendix 8.3). Bit by bit, the private sector's resistance gave way, ineluctably drawing decision makers to accept solutions to the fundamental structural issues that racked the industry. In this process, government increasingly exercised directorial control over business, one form of which was the establishment of cartels. They facilitated a reorganization of the industry directed by government while still according the private sector latitude in the running of the cartel itself.

This is not a story of government imposition but, rather, one of a coordinated business and government response to find a mutually accommodative working solution to the stark realities that confronted them. As we have seen, politicians, bureaucrats and business operated in a comparatively close-knit network. While the zigzagged nature of their prospect paths, the often multi-hat roles played by key actors and their social, economic, and marital ties hemmed them in placing a premium on reputation and trust, strength from financial stakeholding also afforded business—read zaibatsu—independence of action. It was thus that the shift to a new and more strongly coordinative and directorial mode of government and business operation should be seen less as acquiescence and more as acknowledgement that times had changed. Johnson sees the latter half of the 1920s as a turning point from former "self-control" whereby government operated at an arms-length from the market to "state-control" where government centrally managed the economy through the Ministry of Commerce and Industry (MCI) (Johnson, 1982, p. 113).

In this transition, it was, in particular, the 1927 financial crisis that proved to be the "culmination of all the panics that had afflicted the Japanese economy during the 1920s … [and] constitutes the true dividing line between the 'old testament' and the 'new testament' of Japanese trade and industrial administration" (Johnson, 1982, p. 100). Concerns over the fundamentals of the economy and the viability of the banking sector tipped into fear over the government's decision to convert outstanding bills issued following the 1923 Kantō earthquake into ten-year government bonds. Bringing down the

Wakatsuki government, 37 banks went under, tightening loans to small- and medium-sized firms and, in turn, strengthening the position of the zaibatsu.

On the heels of this, MCI set up the Commerce and Industry Deliberation Council on May 23, 1927 and, among its recommendations, urged the amalgamation of the industry. At the same time, the Cabinet independently created on Jun. 2, 1930 the Temporary Industrial Rationality Board that was to formulate and implement industrial policies of rationalization. One of its most important accomplishments was the establishment of the Important Industries Control Law of 1931, the passage of which is seen as pivotal in the transition to this new mode of government and business interaction. The law was written in close consultation with zaibatsu representatives and "constitutes an early instance of the government's providing the auspices for private enterprises to help themselves" (Johnson, 1982, p. 109). In this cooperative spirit akin to what Samuels (1987) calls "Reciprocal Consent," the aim of the law was to accord self-control (jishu tōsei) to the industry, affording it wide latitude in the management of cartels. The intention of this was not the establishment of a self-serving, price-fixing oligopolistic arrangement, but was conceived as a "tool to reduce over-production and inefficient facilities and to realize lower production costs" (Yonekura, 1994, p. 118).

At one level, cartelization was about a cooperative private-public arrangement and also reflected the establishment of a new mindset among bureaucrats and business that provided an ideology to frame solutions to the industry. While being of "considerable rhetorical power," albeit of varied interpreted meanings, rationalization (sangyō gōrika) at its core was the "concept of science" (Tsutsui, 1998, p. 63). Reflecting its intellectual antecedent of Scientific Management, rationalization was about the application of science to industrial problems. This conviction, however, "had more importance as an ideological talisman than as a blueprint for policy" (Tsutsui, 1998, pp. 63–64). Notwithstanding, as will be seen, its acceptance by government and business helped create a common frame of reference in which to discuss the amalgamation of the industry and, in so doing, add impetus to its realization.

Rationalization in 1920s Japan was a hybrid of the industrial reorganization emphasis of German state regulation with the American model "of an undemanding state that coordinated business self-regulation and promoted (rather than dictated) initiatives" (Tsutsui, 1998, p. 64). In this amalgam, cartelization a la 1920s Japan steered from the extremes of state regulation and provided an ideological framework for a new cooperative government and business mode of operation.

In 1925, Kataoka Naoharu, MCI held meetings with his ministry, the Navy and the Finance Ministry to discuss the prospects of consolidation of the iron and steel industry. Concluding that this was unfeasible at the time, he advanced a number of proposals for the establishment of a cartel arrangement to the private sector which "in exchange for accepting these recommendations, demanded … concessions from the government" for financial support, an extension of the Iron and Steel Promotion Law of 1917 and an increase in tariffs on imported iron and steel (Yonekura, 1994, p. 117). This led to the formation of the Iron and Steel Council later that year, and under its aegis, the Pig Iron Cooperative Association in 1926.

In Jan. 1926, under Kataoka's initiative, the proposal was made for an increase in the tariffs on pig iron and steel (Tsūshō Sangyōshō, 1970, p. 241). However, government concerns over trade friction with India stood in the way of the hopes of pig iron producers. In response, subsidization of pig iron was introduced through the revision of the Iron and Steel Promotion Law in Mar. 1926. In rather selective fashion, the outcome of the revised law defined eligibility for subsidization as being those companies that were integrated and had an annual production capacity of over 35,000 tons of iron and steel (Tsūshō Sangyōshō, 1970, p. 243). This subsidization continued until the amalgamation of the industry under Japan Steel in 1934.

Under the control of the Pig Iron Cooperative Association, formed of Kamaishi, Wanishi, Kenjiho, Ben Xi Hua, and Anshan Works, the domestic price of pig iron was stabilized. The association's aims were twofold: (1) stabilization of the market price of pig iron; and (2) setting of the price below Indian pig iron (Yonekura, 1994, p. 126). Declining demand and increased competition, in particular from India, led to a decision to engage in price-fixing without concern to production costs in order to keep Indian pig iron out of Japan. This was possible because of the subsidization given by government to pig iron producers. In addition, an agreement was reached between the Joint Purchase Association of Steelmakers and the Pig Iron Cooperative Association in 1927 whereby steel producers agreed to limit their purchases of Indian pig iron to one-third of their total purchases. In return, the Pig Iron Cooperative would, among other things, adjust the price of its product to that of steel in a ratio of 1:2.2 (Yonekura, 1994, p. 126). Under these conditions, collective price agreements, in combination with the impact on demand due to depression, did reduce the market share of Indian pig iron from 21.9% to 10.6% between 1929 and 1931. However, continued declining prices of steel made the position of the pig iron producers untenable under the agreement and so it was abandoned in 1931 (Iida, 1969, p. 276).

As for steel producers, there was not one encompassing cartel for this sector of the industry, but rather the industry was subdivided between product lines. In 1926, the Bar Segments Agreement was established, which subdivided production according to bar size between Yawata and private sector sites, controlling prices and achieving economies of scale. A similar understanding was achieved for producers of round bars (1927), black plates (1930), wire rods (1930), plates (1931), medium plates (1930), small angles (1931), and medium angles (1931). Though achieving success at controlling prices to varying degrees, none of these associations survived the Shōwa Depression as overall market prices declined (Yonekura, 1994, p. 130).

In the end, although the maintenance of collective price agreements proved to be unsustainable for both pig iron and steel producers, this new arrangement was a departure from the previous mode of operation between government and business in the first half of the 1920s. From the position as an independent actor, business acceded a degree of control to government in return for self-control of the industry.

In Jul. 1932, the issue of tariff increases on pig iron and steel reappeared under the initiative of the Saitō administration. As will be discussed, prevailing conditions helped to facilitate the passage of the bill. Despite strong objections from the Diet, government succeeded in seeing through the legislation. But in the process, the upper chamber strongly insisted that government implement measures for the rationalization of the industry which eventually led to the industry's amalgamation. With the passage of a bill for the increase in tariffs on imported iron and steel in July of 1932, a condition was added by the Upper and Lower Houses that the iron and steel industry must undertake measures to rationalize their facilities (Tsūshō Sangyōshō, 1970, p. 294). This proved to provide the impetus for the final drive to consolidation.

Additionally, as the increase in tariffs placed iron producers in a more favorable position in terms of earning power, they became more open to the idea of consolidation. Prior to the passage of the tariff bill, when their earning capacity was lower, they feared that they would have been in a disadvantaged position when the later evaluation of the assets of those companies participating in the industry amalgamation would have occurred. This fear was allayed by the increase in earning power given the protection through the new tariff and, in turn, iron producers became more willing to consider the merits of amalgamation (Yonekura, 1994, pp. 139–140).

On the political front, recent developments had transpired that helped provide a more favorable environment for the passage of a bill to unify

the industry. Following the May 15 incident, where Prime Minister Inukai Tsuyoshi was assassinated, Saitō Makoto was appointed prime minister. He presided over a so-called "cabinet of national unity" with representatives from the parties, bureaucracy, and military and "it was hoped that Saitō would be able to secure bi-partisan support. This hope was not disappointed: the new cabinet included four men who were associated with the Seiyukai and two from the Minseito" (Sims, 2001, p. 162).

A cabinet of this composite nature was important in providing the bridge between the differences that existed between the parties which facilitated the relatively rapid readings and passage of the bills (Yonekura, 1994, p. 140). Additionally, both Takahashi Korekiyo and Nakajima Kumakichi were ministers of Saitō's cabinet and known for their interest in consolidation, thus providing greater support to the movement (Tsūshō Sangyōshō, 1970, pp. 294–295). In the memoirs of the Nakai Reisaku, "who was designated by Takahashi as Chief Officer of the Yawata Works to carry out the consolidation," the transient nature of the Saitō cabinet created a sense of urgency in the passage of the bill, as "in the party-based cabinets, it had been very difficult to pass for the bill [the consolidation], because when the Seiyukai Cabinet proposed, the Kenseikai opposed, and when the Kenseikai proposed, the Seiyukai was against it" (as cited in Yonekura, 1994, p. 140).

Although there was a sense of urgency, Yonekura Seiichirō argues that "in the Diet, a strong controversy developed over the details of the consolidation, such as its public versus private nature, the method of the asset evaluation, production costs and rationalization, and the management of the consolidated company" (Yonekura, 1994, p. 141). The scope of the examination here does not, for reasons of space, attempt to examine each of the above issues, but focuses on the complaints of pig iron producers. There was ample reason for them to strongly object to the amalgamation plan as stated by Nakajima Kumakichi, the MCI, that "when the plan is in place there will be no need for the system of subsidization for iron and steel industry" (Teikoku Gikai Shūgiin Iinkai, 1989, p. 260).

Though objections were raised, pig iron representatives did present a concerted and forceful challenge to the government position. In other debates where like-minded members rallied together to press the government, or one or two strong spokesmen launched sustained assaults, here, objections were raised, a response provided and then the debate moved on to the next topic without the feeling that the objections would have any impact on the outcome. For example, on Mar. 2, 1933, Matsumoto, a committee member and a spokesman for the pig iron position, challenged the

government's amalgamation plan by challenging the simple notion that by expanding there would necessarily be a reduction in production costs. He claimed that the figures provided did not sustain the government's claims.

In response, Nakai Reisaku responded by making the distinction that he was referring to steel while Matsumoto was speaking of pig iron, and that the focus of the amalgamation plan was steel. He claimed that "pig iron will be bought on a joint basis as a resource ingredient" (Teikoku Gikai Shūgiin Iinkai, 1989, p. 269). Matsumoto complained then about the loss of protection for pig iron producers and Nakai responded with a reiteration of the amalgamation plan's premise of reducing overall production costs, thereby underscoring that the specific pig iron concern was not important. Matsumoto challenged with the observation that though 500 ton furnaces were efficient, the bulk of the industry still used 200 ton furnaces and therefore were inefficient. In response, Nakai admitted that the situation may be more complicated and, essentially, the exchange ended there with Matsumoto asking that an expert determine whether larger furnaces would be cheaper (Teikoku Gikai Shūgiin Iinkai, 1989, p. 269).

In an attempt to answer why pig iron interests were paid so little heed in these debates, perhaps the most determining factor was that integration was about producing steel cheaply and eliminating the inefficiency that was partially attributable to small pig iron producers. Whatever arguments could have been made on the side of the continuation of independent pig iron production, there was little chance that Matsumoto alone would be able to budge the government on this fundamental issue. Moreover, pig iron as an issue was only one among many other issues that were dealt with in discussions. This attitude was reflected in essential as rationale for the amalgamation, which squarely placed priority on national considerations.

As explained by Nakajima, the rationale was twofold: (1) to create efficient steel producing base; and (2) to ensure that Japan had a self-sufficient base for national defense reasons (Teikoku Gikai Shūgiin Iinkai, 1989, p. 259). At a later point in the discussions, Nakajima expanded on the second point when he indicated that the present supply of steel is insufficient, and by expanding the domestic base, it would achieve the end of self-sufficiency which would be critical in the case of war. He stated that this was one important reason why money from the national coffers should be directed to expanding the steel manufacturing capacity to establish the requisite base (Teikoku Gikai Shūgiin Iinkai, 1989, p. 301). Thus we see from the start that the government perspective was national-oriented and not concerned specifically with the welfare of small private sector producers.

The role of the Saitō cabinet, formed of both Seiyūkai and Kenseikai members, was cited in the secondary literature as important in forging the necessary compromise to allow passage of the bill. As we have seen, according to the analysis of Okazaki, amalgamation attempts spearheaded by Takahashi prior to 1925 were thwarted by zaibatsu as they perceived their best interest dictated otherwise. Seen from this perspective, the nature of the Saitō cabinet facilitated the necessary political compromise but, at the same time, the requisite economic circumstances were necessary to make amalgamation of the industry sufficiently compelling.

8.4 CONCLUSION

The relationship between moral persuasion and the shift between modes of exchange is important because, typically, the mandate of government is for change and, as such, the exercise of political skills to realize this change becomes crucial. In terms of institutional restructuring and exchange modes, markets tend to be more stable among developed economies than those still emerging. Market rationale and institutional matrices, become set over time and, for better or worse, accepted by actors. For a country in transition from an agrarian to industrial base, macrostructural change is often necessary to support such plans. Moreover, industrialization among a range of other approaches to economic development is often accompanied by institutional restructuring and, in turn, a shift in the mode of interaction between government and business. This is not to suggest that there is an ideal and prescribed mode of exchange to match the stages and forms of economic development; rather, that relationships spring from and reflect the environment in which they are located.

As Lie points out, the macrostructure frames the context in which a market operates and change provides opportunity for actors to realize ends which do not necessarily coincide. How that political struggle plays itself out is subject to numerous factors, such as the persuasiveness of the moral imperative argument in relation to the changing financial interests of stakeholders. As we have seen in the case of early industrializing Japan, when institutional restructuring of an industry impacts on the interests of actors, ideas in themselves have limited effect in helping government achieve change.

This is not to suggest that ideas—in particular moral ones—are not effective. Our evidence suggests that their persuasiveness derives from their legitimacy in combination with the perceived importance of the

countervailing forces. In this sense, the challenge of government in restructuring and creating a new mode of exchange with business is not just about realizing a positive financial outcome, but also that it be seen as legitimate. It is here in particular that the moral imperative argument realizes its greatest importance. To return to Lie, market transactions are much more than just utility maximization acts; they are embedded in a society and enshrined in the ideological rationale that underpins that society.

APPENDIX 8.1 SHINGIKAI MEETINGS OF THE TEMPORARY INVESTIGATION COMMITTEE ON FISCAL POLICY AND THE ECONOMY

Date	Name
Jul. 9, 1919	Establishment of the Temporary Investigation Committee
Jul. 18, 1919	Temporary Investigation Committee on Fiscal Policy and the Economy—Plenary Session
Nov. 10, 1919	Temporary Investigation Committee on Fiscal Policy and the Economy—Request for Advice Number 3
Nov. 29, 1919– Nov. 8, 1920	Temporary Investigation Committee on Fiscal Policy and the Economy—Record of Special Committee on Requests for Advice Numbers 3 and 4
Feb. 14, 1921	Temporary Investigation Committee on Fiscal Policy and the Economy—Request for Advice Numbers 3 and 4
Feb. 1921	Report on Recommendations of Committee
Mar. 22, 1924	Promulgation of final report

APPENDIX 8.2 BACKGROUND OF LEADING MEMBERS OF THE TEMPORARY INVESTIGATION COMMITTEE ON FISCAL POLICY AND THE ECONOMY

Name	Primary occupation	Background
Hara Kei Chairman	Politician	1895 Deputy Foreign Minister 1897 President of Osaka Mainichi Company 1900–01 Minister of Communications 1902–21 Diet member 1906–08, 1911–12, 1913–14 Home Minister 1918 Prime Minister

Continued

Name	Primary occupation	Background
Takahashi Korekiyo Vice-chairman	Banker Financier Politician	1905 Entered House of Peers (1924 resigned) 1906 President of Yokohama Specie Bank 1911 President of Bank of Japan 1913–14, 1918–21 Finance Minister 1921–22 Prime Minister 1924–25 Agriculture and Commerce Minister 1927, 1931–34, 1934–36, Finance Minister
Yamamoto Tatsuo Vice-chairman	Financier Politician	Employed by Mitsui 1898–1903 President of Bank of Japan 1903 Entered House of Peers 1911 Finance Minister 1913–14, 1921–22 Minister of Agriculture and Commerce
Takahashi Mitsutake Committee Member		Studied law and economics at the University of Cambridge Commissioned by the Ministry of Agriculture and Commerce to conduct research Chief Editor of Osaka Shimbun Chief Secretary of Hara Cabinet 1908 Elected to House of Representatives (re-elected eight times)
Kushida Manzo Committee Member	Banker	1894 Entered 119th Bank 1921 Chairman of the Board of Directors of 109th Bank Numerous positions in Mitsubishi and Mitsui
Hashimoto Keizaburō Committee Member	Businessman Bureaucrat	1890–1913 Held number of prominent positions (head of Yokohama Customs, Vice-minister of Finance and, Agriculture and Commerce) 1912 Entered House of Peers 1916–21 resident of Takarada Oil 1921 Vice-president of Japan Oil
Baron Gō Seinosuke Committee Member	Businessman Financier	1911 Chairman of Tokyo Stock Exchange 1917 Managing Director Industrial Club of Japan 1931 President of National Federation of Industrial Organizations 1932 President of Japan Economic Federation
Count Hayashi Hirotarō Committee Member		1919 Professor at the University of Tokyo 1914–47 Member of House of Peers, participating in numerous committees 1932–35 President of the South Manchurian Railway Company

Name	Primary occupation	Background
Baron Dan Takuma Committee Member	Manager	1888 Director of Mitsui owned Miike Coal Mine 1914–32 General Manager of Mitsui 1916–32 Director Industrial Club of Japan 1928–32 President of Japan Economic Federation
Suzuki Umeshirō Committee Member		Mitsui Bank and Oji Paper Manufacturing Company Editor of Jiji Shimpo
Koyama Kenzo Committee Member	Businessman	1920 Entered House of Peers
Hamaguchi Osachi Committee Member	Politician	Elected to Diet in 1915 1924–26 Finance Minister 1926–27 Home Minister 1927 President of Minseitō 1929 Formed own cabinet
Kajiwara Nakaji Committee Member		1922 (Oct.)–1927 (Oct.) President of Japan Industrial Bank
Yamaoka Juntarō Committee Member		1914 (Mar.)–1926 (Jan.) President of Hitachi Shipbuilding
Yamazaki Kakutarō Committee Member	Academic	Dean of the Department of Economics, Tokyo Imperial University
Yokota Sennosuke Committee Member	Politician	1913 Central role in the second Movement for the Protection of the Constitution 1918 Selected by Hara Kei as Director-General of the Cabinet Legislation Bureau 1924 (Jun.)–1925 (Feb. 5) Minister of Justice
Fujiyama Raita Committee Member	Businessman	1892 Entered Mitsui Bank Held managerial positions in various companies Formed the Fujiyama business group Entered House of Peers

Continued

Name	Primary occupation	Background
Baron Den Kenjirō Committee Member	Bureaucrat Politician	1903 Vice-minister of Communications 1906 Entered House of Peers 1916 Minister of Communications 1919 Governor of Taiwan 1923 Minister of Agriculture and Commerce 1926 Privy Councilor
Inoue Junnosuke Committee Member	Financier Politician	1913 President of Yokohama Specie Bank 1919–23, 1927 Governor of Bank of Japan 1923–24, 1929–31 Minister of Finance
Okazaki Kunisuke Committee Member	Politician	1891 Elected to House of Representative (10 times) 1925 Minister of Agriculture 1928 Entered House of Peers
Kataoka Naoteru	Businessman	Held various leading positions in Osaka located businesses, by Taishō period considered influential member of Osaka financial world. 1918–22 Osaka Industrial Committee chairman Entered House of Peers
Baron Shibusawa Eiichi Committee Member	Businessman	1873 founded First National Bank Noted promoter of industrial and commercial enterprises Major role in introducing Western industries and Western techniques to Japan Maintained advisory role in the business world until his death in 1931

Sources: (1) *Nihon Rekishi Jinbutsu Jiten* (Tokyo: Asahi Shinbunsha, 1994); (2) *Asahi Jinbutsu Jiten* (Tokyo: Asahi Shinbunsha, 1990); (3) Hunter, *Concise Dictionary of Modern Japanese History* (London: University of California Press, 1984).

APPENDIX 8.3 SHINGIKAI MEETINGS ON THE JAPAN STEEL CORPORATION BILL

Date	Name
Mar. 1, 1933–Mar. 11, 1933	Session 64 of Imperial Diet House of Representatives: Proposed Law on the Japan Steel Corporation Committee Records (notes), Readings 1–9
Mar. 16, 1933–Mar. 24, 1933	Session 64 of the Imperial Diet House of Peers: Proposed Law on the Japan Steel Corporation Special Committee Records (notes), Readings 1–7
Nov. 1933	Investigation Committee on the Evaluation of the Iron and Steel Industry Record of the Proceedings of Second Meeting of the Special Committee

REFERENCES

Iida, K. (1969). Tekkō [Iron and steel]. In S. Ōhashi & T. Kuroiwa (Eds.), *Gendai Nihon Sangyō Hattatsu Shi [History of modern Japan industrial development]*. Tokyo: Kojunsha.
Johnson, C. (1982). *MITI and the Japanese miracle: The growth of industrial policy, 1925–1975*. Tokyo: Charles E. Tuttle Co.
Lie, J. (1992). The concept of mode of exchange. *American Sociological Review*, 57(4), 508–523.
Okazaki, T. (1984). 1920 Nendai No Tekkōgyō Seisaku to Nihon Tekkōgyō—Seitetsu Gōdō Mondai O Chūshin Toshite [1920s Iron and steel strategy and Japan's iron and steel industry the amalgamation of the iron and steel industry]. *Tochi Seido Shi Gaku [History of the Land System]*, 103, 1–18.
Rinji zaisei keizai chōsakai [Temporary Committee on Finance and Economics] (Ed.), (1919). *Shimon Dai San Gō Oyobi Dai Yon Gō Tokubetsu Iinkai Gijiroku [Records of the special committee numbers 35 and 45]*. Tokyo: Kokuritsu Kōbun Shokan (reference number 2A 36 268).
Samuels, R. (1987). *The Business of the Japanese state: Energy markets in comparative and historical perspective*. Ithaca, NY: Cornell University Press.
Samuels, R. (1994). *Rich nation, strong army: National security and the technological transformation of Japan*. Ithaca, NY: Cornell University Press.
Sims, R. (2001). *Japanese political history since the Meiji renovation 1869–2000*. London: Hurst & Company.
Teikoku Gikai Shūgiin Iinkai [Committee Meeting of the Imperial Diet House of Representatives] (Eds.), (1989). *Nihon Seitetsu Kabushiki Kaisha Hōritsuan Iinkai Gijiroku Dai Ikkai~Dai Kyū Kai [Records of the committee on the proposed law on Japan steel corporation]—1933 Dai 64 Kai Teikoku Gikai [Diet 44], Teikoku Gikai Shūgiin Iinkai Giroku [Records of the imperial diet house of representatives]*. Kyoto: Rinsen Shoten.
Tsūshō Sangyōshō [Ministry of International Trade and Industry] (Ed.), (1970). *Shōkō Seisakushi: Tekkōgyō [The history of commercial and industrial policy: the iron and steel industry]*, 17, Shōkō Seisakushim [The history of commercial and industrial policy]. Tokyo: Shōkō Seisakushi Kankokai.
Tsutsui, W. (1998). *Manufacturing ideology: Scientific management in twentieth-century Japan*. Princeton, NJ: Princeton University Press.
Yonekura, S. (1994). *The Japanese steel industry, 1850–1990: Continuity and discontinuity*. London: Macmillan Press Ltd.

CHAPTER 9

Political Economy of Business Ethics in East Asia

I. Oh, G.-S. Park
Korea University, Seoul, South Korea

9.1 INTRODUCTION

A big question that is raised by this book deals with the validity of a Eurocentric thesis that business ethics is a product of Western modernization as a terminal result of the capitalist evolution into the current global free market economies. Furthermore, another relevant question was whether debunking is possible for an evolutionary thesis that the current global free market economy is epitomized by voluntary ethical coordination among state, business, and workplace actors. Authors of the chapters in this volume asked these two questions against both historical and contemporary cases from East Asia to see if longitudinal and latitudinal data would reveal any validity in the assertion that modes of exchange and modes of moral persuasion in business have any linear evolutionary trajectory with a terminal stage in the form of the global free market economy.

The chapters in this volume ambitiously examine a variety of historical and contemporary facets of the political economy of business ethics. After setting up a theoretical cornerstone using Lie's modes of exchange and Oh's modes of moral persuasion in the political economy of business ethics, Baumann and Winzar take up the case of East Asian Confucianism in order to demonstrate the fact that Confucian moral persuasion and modes of exchange can persist in the 21st century Asia, despite the presence of competing economic ideologies, including global free market capitalism. What was intriguing about the Confucian work ethic was the fact that economic efficiency in fact can increase substantially in the service sector, if the Confucian or manorial mode of exchange is upheld in lieu of market or entrepreneurial modes of exchange. Furthermore, they found that Confucian education as a manorial form of moral persuasion for economic actors was pivotal in leading East Asian countries as champions of economic growth and competitiveness.

On the other hand, Park's chapter contended that Confucian or manorial modes of exchange within the Korean big corporations or the *chaebol* subsided ostensibly with the inundation of the Western modes of exchange and/or moral persuasion, namely pro-market or pro-entrepreneurial business ethics. New agents of change, including civil liberty groups and Nongovernmental Organizations (NGOs), were brought to the forefront at the moderation of corporate and state authoritarianism. Minority shareholder activism that demanded grassroots participation in the corporate decision making to enhance transparencies of corporate governance and the state-business relations was the byproduct of economic transformation, which was consolidated further by the political demise of military autarky to civil democracy. However, Park also admits to the limitations of Western style economic reforms, given the harnessing effect of the resilient institutions and their moral persuasions that tout the efficiencies of previous regimes and institutions.

As an extension to Park's conclusion on Korean business ethics in the 21st century, Dalton and dela Rama pursue the difficult task of unpacking an enigma surrounding the *chaebol* succession issue. The authors' intention was to highlight the obvious moral dilemma rampant in Korean society: that the *chaebol* or the state wouldn't give up their social, economic, and political power, despite the massive political and economic reforms that have occurred in Korea since the 1997 Asian financial crisis. Notably weighty and therefore obtrusive to anyone in Korean society is the question of how to hand down one's property to his son, a practice that is the very lynchpin of Confucian filial piety and patriarchy. Despite the fact that the *chaebol*, in tandem with the developmental state, had successfully maintained its ideal image as promoters of economic well-being for Korea in the past, competing norms of transparency and the state legal measures of anticorruption that introduced hefty inheritance taxes ensued a new moral dilemma for *chaebol* families. Typical in many historical cases, strict legal institutions that regulate business ethics would certainly provide chaebol families with new motivations to introduce countermeasures that would be construed as illegitimate by many. In this sense, Confucian or manorial modes of exchange and moral persuasion can work either as an efficient means of promoting productivity or as a morally bankrupt means of fortifying traditional management practices.

Howard's chapter further illustrates the question of the chaotic coexistence of different modes of exchange and moral persuasion in Korean society, using the case of K-pop. The choice of music industry in fact clearly

served the purpose of this book by illustrating why the music industry in Korea had been a target of close state control in terms of its content, unlike the conventional view that it belongs to the category of a typical free market mode of exchange, where profit maximization is possible only by satisfying music listeners' taste. The case demonstrated that the entire music industry in Korea had been under close scrutiny by state authorities who feared the possibility of a "demoralized" public. The music industry, therefore, had been a government showcase of ethical control until the entire industry was liberalized and globalized. Howard found that liberalization and globalization did not really develop the Korean entertainment industry into a full-fledged recording industry as in an Anglo-American fashion. Global gatekeepers in the music industry appeared as a new regulator, and this made the entire K-pop industry a subcontractor of the big three global recording labels and other distributors. Therefore, the mercantilist mode of exchange under the Korean dictatorship is now supplemented with the entrepreneurial mode as well.

The two historical cases of Joseon Korea and Taishō and Shōwa Japan, contributed by Kang, and Choi and von Staden, respectively, provided a longitudinal angle to this study, as chapter authors narrated how competing modes of exchange and moral persuasions worked as institutional bulwarks against competition norms imported from the West during the first and second phases of East Asian modernization. Eighteenth century Joseon faced severe economic and political devastations due to internal famines, economic meltdowns, and dangers of foreign invasions from China, Japan, and the West. To counter these internal and external threats, Joseon came up with a brilliant idea of offering a market-based Confucian welfarism that tried to ease peasants' tax burdens and the hardships of the urban poor. Under the strict institutional norms of manorial (or Confucian) and mercantilist (or Confucian state) modes of exchange and moral persuasions, the government nonetheless allowed small-scale markets where peasants could sell their surplus products directly (i.e., market mode), whereas merchants could raise enormous profits by interregional trade (i.e., entrepreneurial mode), which were then taxed to help the urban poor. This way, the government could still rely on the mercantilist mode of exchange by purchasing their daily necessaries from the monopoly suppliers (or *yukeuijeon*).

The Japanese historical case represents the origin of the developmental state in East Asia, whose purport was to master the process of industrial planning with a new moral slogan of "a wealthy nation with a strong army [*fukoku kyōhei*]." Using some of the *shingikai* data, von Staden demonstrates

that the Japanese developmental state systematically used methods of moral persuasion in order to justify the amalgamation of the iron and the steel industries. While promoting entrepreneurialism during modernization, it is apparent that Japan also envisaged a more centralized and plan-savvy government that could also compete with leading Western states with far more advanced apparatuses of industrial development and military clout. In line with Lie's arguments on the mercantilist mode, von Staden's historical case thus substantiates the institutional and social origin of the mode of exchange.

Given these empirical findings, we can arrive at theoretical implications on business ethics in premodern and modern macro and micro economic institutions.

9.2 THEORETICAL IMPLICATIONS OF THE FINDINGS

The political economy of business ethics posits that business ethics is heavily controlled and managed by the political, against the common belief that it is voluntarily implemented and enforced by the market, business corporations, and entrepreneurs. Our premodern and modern case studies of East Asia in general, and Korea and Japan in particular suggest that business ethics in East Asia has been in existence for many centuries, being manipulated by both business and state actors in their attempt to advance their own interests or defend their macro-political institutions. Competing norms or ideas of business ethics, like those for the political institutions themselves, have coexisted throughout different epochs of history in East Asia. The reason for coexistence is none other than the need of the political to defend its own institutional *raison d'être* by tenaciously upholding its political ideals while transforming the economy more frequently than their efforts at reforming politics. Therefore, the political economy of business ethics is about deploying ethics to the forefront of business and political discourse in order to satisfy the discontent of the public that demands sweeping political reforms that would automatically ensue economic overhaul.

In this regard, John Lie's concept of modes of exchange is a complete theoretical departure from the neoliberal and market essentialist discourse, which even Polanyi (1944) failed to achieve. In addition, Lie's model best serves our purpose of defining and explaining business ethics as a fluid concept that changes frequently depending on the needs of justifying economic

and political actors' policies. Therefore, if we add modes of persuasion to modes of exchange, we start to be able to make out a complete picture of the political economic evolution of premodern and modern economic institutions. What has not been studied thoroughly in this volume is how modes of persuasion correspond to modes of exchange. For example, the Confucian (manorial) mode of exchange, could have necessitated the Confucian (manorial) mode of persuasion. However, historical cases reveal that people in power often used force or similar means to reform economic institutions, despite the fact that they deployed moral persuasions on a putatively symbolic level. We therefore need to know why symbolic discourse of moral persuasions are needed in institutional transitions not only in East Asia but in other parts of the world, despite the fact that force itself is sufficient to effect changes.

Nonetheless, modes of exchange and moral persuasions provide us with a valuable insight for the explanation and understanding of East Asian business ethics as a political economic process of enacting changes within the economic to defend the political. Without these notions, we have often fallen into the trap of accepting Eurocentric arguments that business ethics exists as a final stage of capitalism that is found only in advanced European and North American societies.

9.3 METHODOLOGICAL WISDOM IN THE STUDY OF ECONOMIC HISTORY AND BUSINESS ETHICS

Business ethics studies have long adopted a self-defeating strategy of investigating national and international state of ethical standings: quantifying ethical standards and practices of business in each country (Randall & Gibson, 1990). As we tried to show in this volume, an important aspect of all business ethics research is to discover the political economic logic of manipulating business ethics, not in terms of how to quantify and rank each country in terms of their ethical practices. To do this, we need to be able to unsubscribe to theories of "ought" (e.g., East Asian business ought to follow the Anglo-American model, etc.) or methodologies of standardization, but instead use "ethical imaginations" (Park, 1998) to locate the political economic fundamentals of business ethics amid various cultural and historical variations.

A prominent methodological means of investigating cross-cultural and cross-sectional variations of ethical practices would be to employ

comparative and historical methods. In this book we used comparative and historical methods within a closed set of East Asian variations, or the method of similarities. Assuming that all East Asian nations are culturally and historically similar, our expected result of the method of similarities was to find differences between East Asian cases. Indeed, Korea differed from Japan substantially in that the latter state used more persuasive tactics than the coercive means that the Korean state utilized. Furthermore, Korea displayed the tendency of harshly enforcing new ethical norms to eradicate old practices more than Japan, which tried to find an equilibrium of harmonious coexistence between old and new norms. Nevertheless, the historical comparative method revealed fundamental commonalities as well in the sense that all East Asian states tend to maintain Confucianism as a means of defending and justifying corporations' self-interests. The institution of first son succession is a Confucian value, but it is also a very selfish norm.

9.4 FUTURE GUIDELINES FOR BUSINESS ETHICS RESEARCH

A typical Eurocentric approach to business ethics research is to test normative criteria of behavior (i.e., what is "ought" to be done?) against quantified value data (i.e., how many standardized behaviors are observed in one test?) (Robertson, 1993). However, as this book has shown, this type of research endangers the whole system of knowledge we call business ethics. First and foremost, ethics cannot be dictated upon human beings in organizations from above. What was ethically correct in the 18th century Korea is no longer a valid norm in the 21st century Korea. Furthermore, what was ethically correct in 20th century France cannot be valid any in 21st century Germany. Therefore, ethical dictation is the very act of moral practice that needs to be empirically studied, including Eurocentric studies of business ethics.

Future studies of business ethics need to focus on the political economic mechanism of ethical practices and dictation. In so doing we need to analyze who gets benefits of ethical practices performed by business actors at large. Empirical components of future studies of business ethics will only be about how to find commonalities and differences between political economic institutions of ethical dictations found in each country. Historical and comparative studies of business ethics will be very beneficial in locating such similarities and differences.

REFERENCES

Park, H.-J. (1998). Can business ethics be taught?: A new model of business ethics education. *Journal of Business Ethics, 17,* 965–977.

Polanyi, K. (1944). *The great transformation: The political and economic origins of our time.* Boston, MA: Beacon Press.

Randall, D., & Gibson, A. (1990). Methodology in business ethics research: A review and critical assessment. *Journal of Business Ethics, 9,* 457–471.

Robertson, D. (1993). Empiricism in business ethics: Suggested research directions. *Journal of Business Ethics, 12,* 585–599.

INDEX

Note: Page numbers followed by *f* indicate figures and *t* indicate tables.

A
Anticorruption, 84
Antimaterialism, 86
Asian financial crisis, 72–73, 88, 91–92
Audio soundtracks, 104

B
Balanced incomplete block (BIB) design, 52, 53*t*
Bankruptcy, 135
Bar Segments Agreement, 141
Business ethics, 75–76, 79
　business ethics research, guidelines for, 156
　and economic history, 155–156
　macro-level norms of, 7–8
　political and economic transition, 82
Business groups, 88

C
Capitalism, 16, 62–63, 113–114
Capitalist market economy, 18–19
Censorship, 97–100
Chinese Cultural Values (CCV), 34
Chinese Value Survey, 52
Colonial censorship, 99
Columbia Graphophone Company, 97–98
Commerce and Industry Deliberation Council, 139
Committee membership, 135
Commodity exchange, 15–16, 18–19, 22–27
Communication, 24–25
Confucian goodwill, 6, 115, 119–120, 126–128
Confucianism, 7, 85–87
　Confucian competitive strategies, 47*t*
　Confucian culture, 34
　Confucian dynamism, 52–54
　humanistic tradition, 86
　and Korean folk traditions, 87
　policy and practice, 50
　ReVaMB model, 35–46
　values/behavior research, 49–50
　in workplace, 46–48
Confucian philosophy, 35–36
Confucian values, 54–55
　of antimaterialism, 86
　face saving, 55
　group orientation, 55
　hierarchy, 55
　humility, 55
　reciprocity, 55
Confucian virtues, 87
Confucian work ethic (CWE), 34, 39, 46, 48–52
　career stages, 41
　and commitment, 42
　Confucian diligence and harmony, 52
　performance, 42
　psychology and human resource management, 40
Corporate authoritarianism, 8
　company owner's method of management, 62
　Daewoo conglomerate, 61
　1997 financial crisis, 61, 63
　fraudulent accounting, 61
　IMF, 63
　investment risks, 62–63
　Korean self-identity, 63
　Korea's banks, bankruptcy of, 61–62
　market power, 62–63
　unilateral authoritarian politics, 64
Corporate governance
　Asian countries, 72–73, 72*t*, 74*t*
　and business ethics post-financial crises, 88–89
　company stakeholders, welfare of, 64
　financial crisis, 71–72
　IMF's governance, 72–73
　PSPD, 66–67
　shareholder-centric corporate governance structure, 65
　structure, 69–71, 70*t*

Corporate governance structure
  corporate governance reforms, 71
  1997 financial crisis, 75
  internal organization of companies, 69–71
  minority shareholders' rights, 69, 70*t*
Corporate social responsibility (CSR), 1
Corruption, 82
Cultural difference theory, 43
Cultural dimensions model, 43

D

Daedongbeop, 114–115, 127–128
  Confucian goodwill, 119–120
  enforcement of, 116
  financial resources, 119
  fiscal policy, 117
  implementation, 116, 119
  and market dynamism, 120–121
  state managerial ethics and market perceptions, 121–127
  structure and guiding principles, 118–119, 118*f*
  taxation equality, 116, 118–120
  tributary system, 116–118
Direct trade, 26–27

E

East Asia
  economic growth, 33–34
  education, 33–34
  filial piety, 7
  manorial and mercantile modes of exchange, 6
  market/entrepreneurial mode of exchange, 6
  migration of, 33
Ethical persuasion, 3–6, 4*t*, 6*t*

F

Feudalism, 113–114
Financial crisis, 61, 63, 73, 75, 138–139
Financial market, 17–18
Fiscal policy, 115, 117
Free market discourses, 1
Free market economy, 3–4

G

Gaisberg, Fred, 97–98
German Beka-Record company, 97–98

Global music industry, 9–10, 95
Gross domestic product (GDP), 12
Group orientation, 55

H

Horne, F.W., 97–98
Human economic history, 1–2
Human resource management, 40

I

Ideology, 132, 139
Indirect trade, 26
Institute of Management Development (IMD), 73, 74*t*
Institutional evolution, 1
Institutional restructuring, 137, 144
International Federation of Phonographic Industries (IFPI), 95–96, 104–105, 109
International Monetary Fund (IMF), 63, 68, 72–73, 88
Internet, 25
Interregional trade, 2
Intraregional trade, 2
Ipsative measure, 51
Iron and steel industry (1919–34), 11, 131–132
  entrepreneurial mode of exchange, 133–137
  mercantile mode of exchange, 138–144
Iron and Steel Promotion Law, 140

J

Japan, 132
  domestic and foreign policies, 133
  Japanese recording companies, 98–99
  moral persuasions, 6
Japan Steel Corporation Bill, 148–149
Joseon, 113, 127–128
  Daedongbeop, principle of, 116–121
  fiscal policy, 115
  managerial ethics, 115
  market policies, 125
  political and economic capabilities, 113–114
  redistribution economy, 114
  Seonhyecheong, management of, 116–121

K
Kantian ethics, 3
Korea
   chaebol, 79–86, 88–92, 152
   chaebol legitimacy problem, 9
   competitive political process, 83
   Confucian values, 8
   corporate authoritarianism, 61–64
   corporate governance, 8
   corporate governance structure, changes in, 69–71
   corruption charges, 83–84
   cultural traditions, 79–80
   economic and political elites, 9
   economic and social transformation, 80
   entertainment companies, 97
   fraudulent accounting, 61–64
   justice system, 85
   Korea Development Institute, 89
   Korean capitalism, 8
   Korean culture, 85–88
   Korean self-identity, 63
   manorial mode of exchange, 6
   minority shareholders' movement, 64–69
   mixed modes of exchange, 80–81
   moral persuasions, 6
   music industry, 9–10
   NGO activities, 8
   political corruption, 83–84
   postwar economic development, 80
   public sector mechanisms, lack of, 8
   state bureaucrats, 81
Korea Music Copyright Association (KOMCA), 103
Korean Broadcasting Review Committee, 100–101
Korean music industry
   ballads, 103–105
   colonial period to 1945, 97–100
   postliberation, 1945–1992, 100–103
Korean pop (K-pop), 10, 95–96, 152–153
   export potential in, 108–109
   High Five of Teenagers (H.O.T.), 105–107
   JYP Entertainment and YG Entertainment, 106
   SM Entertainment, 105–106, 108–109
Korean Public Performances Screening Committee, 100–101
Korean War, 80, 100–101
K-pop. *See* Korean pop (K-pop)

L
Labor market, 16–17, 22

M
Macroeconomic institutions, 1, 5
Managers, 81, 90–91
Market
   capitalist market economy, 18–19
   category of, 15
   commodification, 21–23
   definition, 16–17
   domestic market, 135
   financial market, 17–18
   government-licensed merchants, 122–125
   government's procurement method, 122
   and grain loan system, 126
   interdisciplinary approach, 18
   labor market, 16–17, 22
   market-based Confucian welfarism, 153
   market economy, 15–16, 21–22
   market exchange, 24–25
   market socialism, 16
   and mode of exchange, 23–29
   neoclassical market, 21
   Polanyi, Karl, 19–23
   public livelihood and state redistribution, 126
   in Seoul, 123–124
   Smith, Adam, 19–23
   social relations and social structures, 18
   and state managerial ethics, 121–127
Market authority, 76
Market economy, 68
Marxism, 16
Media, 101–106
Methodology, 155–156
Microeconomic institutions, 5
Ministry of Commerce and Industry (MCI), 138–140, 142
Minority shareholders' movement
   business executives, administrative practices of, 65
   capital market, 65
   companies' structural adjustment, principles for, 68
   financial crisis, 64–65, 67

Minority shareholders' movement (*Continued*)
    funding source, 67
    labor unions, 67
    NGOs, 64–65
    PSPD, 65–68
    shareholder-centric corporate governance structure, 65
Mode of moral persuasion. *See* Moral persuasion
Moderator, 45
Modes of exchange, 79, 121, 131, 144, 154–155
    agenda, 29–30
    communication, 24–25
    direct trade, 26–27
    entrepreneurial mode, 29, 81, 133–137
    historical movements, 5
    indirect trade, 26
    institutional changes, 4
    intraregional and interregional trade, 2, 5, 26
    Korean development, 80–81
    macro- and microeconomic institutions, 5
    macro-structural changes, 25
    manorial mode, 27–28, 80
    market mode, 27, 81
    mercantile mode, 28, 80–81, 138–144
    music industry, 97
    opportunity structures, 4
    perfect market, 3–4
    social networks, 4
    social relations of exchange, 24–26
    succession planning, 89–91
    territorial and institutional restrictions, 4
    transportation, 24–25
Moral persuasion, 144, 151–155
Multidimensional work ethic profile (MWEP), 56, 56*t*

N

Non-governmental Organizations (NGOs), 8, 64–65, 73, 152
Normative measure, 37–39, 48

P

Pedagogical approaches, 33–34, 41, 50
People's Solidarity for Participatory Democracy (PSPD)
    Cheil Bank's illegal loans and criminal actions, 65–66
    delegation of shares, 67
    domestic institutional investors, 67
    Kia Motors shares, 66–67
    Samsung Electronics, convertible bonds, 66
Perfect competition, 3
Personality, 44
Pig Iron Cooperative Association, 140
Polanyi, Karl, 19–23
Political authority, 133, 135
Political dynamics, 137
Political economy, 16, 19–20, 22, 29–30, 151, 154
Private sector, 132, 134–136, 138, 140–141, 143
Professionalism, 91–92
Programme for International Student Assessment (PISA), 33–34
Protestant work ethic (PWE), 40, 49
Psychology, 40

R

Rationalization, 133–144
Rawlsian ethics, 3
Recorded music industry, 95–97, 109
Redistribution economy, 114
Relationalism, 39
Relative values, 51–56, 53*t*
Relative values and moderated behavior (ReVaMB) model, 7*f*, 43*f*
    career stage, 46
    competitive/cooperative, 45
    Confucian work ethic, 40–42
    family-owned/ employee, 45
    generalized conceptual framework, 35*f*
    indigenous/foreign-multinational, 45
    interpersonal influences, 45
    life experiences, 44
    personality, 44
    personal values, 35–39
    society, 43–44

workplace behavior, 39
World Values Survey, 36–37, 38*f*
Republic of Korea, 100–101

S

Seonhyecheong, 114–115, 127
   management of, 116–121
   and market dynamism, 120–121
   procurement pricing, 124
Service provision, 39
Smith, Adam, 19–23
Socialism, 16
Succession planning, 89–91

T

Taxation equality, 116, 118–120
Tax collection system, 116
Temporary Industrial Rationality Board, 139
Temporary Investigation Committee on Fiscal Policy and the Economy
   members, background of, 134, 145–148
   shingikai meetings of, 134, 145
Transportation, 24–25

U

Uniform Land Tax, 114–115, 119–120
US financial market, 17
Utilitarianism, 3

V

Videos, 104, 108

W

The Wealth of Nations, 20–21
Work ethic, 41*t*
   antecedent factors, 42–44
   career stage, 41, 46
   and commitment, 42
   high-context and low-context cultures, 44–45
   implications, 49
   MWEP, 56, 56*t*
   organization type, 45
   psychology and human resource management, 40
   PWE, 40
   social norms, organization, 45
World Bank, 89
World Economic Forum (WEF), 73, 74*t*
World Values Survey (WVS), 36–37, 38*f*

Printed in the United States
By Bookmasters